P9-BBO-359

Praise for Deborah Reber and *Doable*

"*Doable* inspires and equips girls to be powerful authors in their own lives."

Alexis Jones, founder of I AM THAT GIRL

"*Doable* is relevant, relatable, and filled with AWESOME resources to help you accomplish "real time" goals and big time dreams! If you follow these Doable steps, you will have coached yourself to live a life you truly love."

Tami Walsh, president/founder of TeenWisdom.com

"I love this book! Life can be overwhelming at any age, but *Doable* provides a positive and encouraging way forward. Don't make the mistake of thinking this is merely a self-help book. It's a make-it-happen, get-it-done, and feel great about tomorrow book."

Chris Guillebeau, *New York Times* bestselling author of *The $100 Startup*

"My daughter is only six, but I am already reading her passages from *Doable*. Debbie is the perfect coach, guide, and mentor to ensure our teen girls love their lives, and grow into strong, confident women."

Pamela Slim, author of *Body of Work*

"I love this book! I dare you to read it and not feel totally inspired to go out into the world and own it. This book will give you the tools to set and accomplish goals, figure out who you are and what matters to you, and face your fears."

Rachel Simmons, author of *The Curse of the Good Girl* and *Odd Girl Out*

"*Doable* is a smart, clear guide with actionable advice. The book shows girls that any goal is within reach!"

Melissa Walker, author of *Ashes to Ashes* and *Unbreak My Heart*

"If you love a teen, buy her this book. Inspiring, engaging, and full of action-packed advice, *Doable* is the ultimate teen playbook for turning goals into reality."

Samantha Ettus, bestselling author and *Forbes* contributor and radio host

"What I love about *Doable* is that it offers a goal-pursuing approach that leverages the readers' unique strengths so she doesn't have to change who she is to get what she wants. Author Debbie Reber shows us that when girls truly understand their own doable style, any goal becomes attainable!"

Dr. Robyn Silverman, teen development expert, speaker, and author

"Calling all girls: *Doable* gives you *everything* you need to know to take actions to find your power, live your dreams and then dream bigger."

Denise Restauri, author, *Forbes* contributor, and founder and CEO of GirlQuake

doable

The Girls' Guide to Accomplishing Just About Anything

DEBORAH REBER

Simon Pulse
New York London Toronto Sydney New Delhi

Hillsboro, Oregon

An imprint of Simon & Schuster
Children's Publishing Division
1230 Avenue of the Americas
New York, NY 10020

20827 N.W. Cornell Road, Suite 500
Hillsboro, Oregon 97124-9808
503-531-8700 / 503-531-8773 fax
www.beyondword.com

This Beyond Words/Simon Pulse edition January 2015

Front cover illustration by Karina Granda

Managing Editor: Lindsay S. Brown
Editors: Nicole Geiger, Ali McCart, Emmalisa Sparrow
Copyeditor: Ashley Van Winkle
Proofreader: Michelle Blair
Interior design: Sara E. Blum
Cover design: Karina Granda
The text of this book was set in Avenir.

Manufactured in the United States of America

10 9 8 7 6 5 4 3 2 1

Library of Congress Cataloging-in-Publication Data

Reber, Deborah.
  Doable : the girls' guide to accomplishing just about anything / Deborah Reber.
    pages cm
  1. Success—Juvenile literature. 2. Success in adolescence—Juvenile literature.
    3. Motivation (Psychology)—Juvenile literature. 4. Teenage girls—
    Psychology—Juvenile literature. I. Title.
BF724.3.S9R43 2015
158.0835'2—dc23

2014005614

ISBN 978-1-58270-467-8 (hc)
ISBN 978-1-58270-466-1 (pbk)
ISBN 978-1-4814-0330-6 (eBook)

To my sweet son, Asher,
who is fueled by intense creativity
and the belief that anything and
everything is possible.

CONTENTS

1
THE DOABLE WAY

Alison is a junior in high school. She has a regular volunteer gig, a slew of babysitting clients, a full load of college prep classes, a spot on the varsity field hockey team, and an active social life. Oh yeah, she's also on the school's environmental Green Team, has weekly chores at home, dreams of starting her own nonprofit this year to help rescue shelter dogs, and has her sights set on getting into a small, liberal arts college in New England.

Alison is the epitome of a classic overachiever—someone who outperforms expectations. And even if that's not how you would describe yourself, my hunch is that you have a lot in common with her. Like Alison, you have big dreams, things you need to take care of every day, longer-term goals you're reaching for, and a busy, *busy* life. (Am I right?)

Busy Much?

Having a To Do list a mile long—whether it's full of huge aspirations or mundane little tasks—just seems to be how teens roll these days. Perhaps more than any other generation before you, you've got full lives, full schedules, and a ton of things to do. So the question is, how good are you at getting stuff done?

Perhaps some To Dos are a piece of cake for you, while just the thought of doing others makes you break out in hives. Perhaps getting just about anything completed is challenging for you, so much so that you've started doubting your own ability to tackle and accomplish anything of importance. Maybe you've come up with your own way of tracking what's on your plate, be it jotting down your tasks on scraps of paper or putting them in a memo app on your phone. Wherever you fall on the continuum, there's no doubt that successfully tackling To Dos involves a lot more than just writing down what needs to be done and then doing it. If it were that easy, we'd all be super productive, procrastination wouldn't exist, our stress levels would be close to zero, and frankly, this book would never have been published.

One of the things people ask me all the time is how I manage to get so much done. Because, like you, I have a lot on my plate. I mean, I have a nine-year-old son who requires a lot of energy and patience to parent, I volunteer regularly, I exercise (nearly) every day, I take care of the house (clean, cook, laundry, and so on), and as of the writing of this book, I had just relocated to Amsterdam in the Netherlands with my family. Plus, I coach writers and creative entrepreneurs, consult on a number of writing projects including a website for teens and a television show for preschoolers, and write books for a living.

So yes, getting it all done is something I've become super good at, whether I'm shipping a completed manuscript or clearing out a closet. Some people are experts at starting businesses, developing computer games, or performing life-saving surgeries. Me? I cross things off my To Do list like nobody's business.

Teen Dreams

When I first began researching this book, I talked to many teen girls just like you and asked them what they wished they could do but had trouble doing. As you can imagine, I got all kinds of answers. Here are just a few:

- Get good grades
- Make an impact and be known for my passions
- Go to school to learn sign language and be an interpreter for a child
- Generate more school spirit on campus
- Make a documentary
- Become an animator
- Get a job at a law firm during high school
- Find the funds to do nonprofit work without worrying about where I'm going to get money to take care of myself
- Turn things in when they're due instead of being late all the time

- Learn how to surf

- Tell the guy I like that I like him

- Find time for me

Next, I asked these girls what *big* dreams they would pursue if they knew with 100 percent certainty that they would be successful. These were some of my favorite answers:

- Go to Harvard

- Be an actress

- Make my own talk show

- Be a professional violinist

- Teach photography or writing

- Make my own fashion line

- Be the best softball player I could be

- Apply to Columbia University

- Build wells in Africa

- Get my wildlife rehabilitation license

Lastly, I asked these teens what it was that regularly got in their way and thwarted their attempts to do what they set out to do. Here's where I discovered what was preventing these awesome girls from kicking serious booty in their lives:

inter··rup··tions

- I lose momentum if I have any setbacks.
- I have a really hard time starting and finishing things, and since I expect I won't be able to do it, I don't even bother trying.
- I don't know whether I'll be successful or not.
- A lot of times, goals just end up being so big or intense that I literally don't believe I have what it takes.
- I get distracted and lose interest.
- I'm uncomfortable taking risks.
- I don't have enough time to do it on top of everything else I have going on.
- I don't actually have a strategy for goal setting and goal pursuing.

- I'm so overtired I don't have any energy left to accomplish my goals.

- I have low self-esteem.

- I don't have enough information to begin.

Any of these answers ring a bell? Good. Because this book you're holding in your hot little hands contains my best secrets and tips for addressing all these problems and more. My goal? To help you be as productive as you want to be. To turn any goal or pursuit into a doable venture.

Don't worry . . . I'm not going to tell you that you have to stick to some intimidating, intricate plan for my approach to work. And *Doable* isn't about figuring out everything you're doing wrong and fixing that. (That doesn't sound like a very good read!) In fact, I believe you already have absolutely everything you need to be successful at getting things done. It's true. You have what it takes—your unique strengths, your gifts, your talents . . . your essence. *Doable* is about discovering, unlocking, and ultimately harnessing all of these by plugging them into a framework that can be applied to any (seriously . . . *any*) To Do. By exploring and consequently understanding your own beliefs, thoughts, experiences, and style, you get to know your biggest asset . . . *you!* That's the benefit of self-knowledge, and it's the key to success on any level—just ask the queen of self-discovery, Oprah, who has built a global media empire rooted in helping people learn how to be their best selves. When you know how you best operate in any circumstance, you can figure out what you need in order to get anything done.

Doable in Eight Steps

Over the following chapters, I'll share with you my eight-step approach for making anything doable, but here's a sneak peak:

Step 1: Define Your To Do: Get crystal clear on exactly what you want to do and why you want to do it.

Step 2: Detail the Little Tasks: Break your goal down into the smallest possible parts.

Step 3: Defend Against Obstacles: Recognize the obstacles that often get in your way and plan for them ahead of time.

Step 4: Develop Support Systems: Harness all available resources—tangible, emotional, and otherwise—to support you.

Step 5: Determine What Success Looks Like: Know exactly what it will feel and look like to have achieved your goal.

Step 6: Do the Work: Dive in and get down to the business of doing.

Step 7: Deal with Setbacks: Expect, embrace, and learn from the failures and setbacks you experience along the way.

Step 8: Deliver the Goods: See your goal pursuit through to completion, and then acknowledge, celebrate, and reflect on the journey.

See what I mean? This isn't brain science. It's straightforward. It's practical. And best of all, it works. Apply these steps in your own unique way to anything on your To Do list and you'll be on your way to getting it done. Boom.

Oh, that reminds me: everyone who reads this book will be working toward different things. Some will be chasing huge dreams, like earning a pilot's license or auditioning for a Broadway play. Others might have straightforward goals like landing an internship. And some might want to tackle day-to-day To Dos, like emptying the cat litter or feeding Fido, with more ease. But here's the thing: it doesn't matter what we're talking about—To Dos, goals, or dreams—they're all doable. So I'll interchange these terms freely throughout this book.

To get the most out of *Doable*, go through it chapter by chapter, as each step builds on the previous and contributes to the overall goal of accomplishing anything you set out to do. To take it a step further, go to www.debbiereber.com and download the free accompanying *Doable* workbook so you can put the steps to the test by applying them to your own life and To Dos. Or if you're more of a journal girl, that works too. Whatever your method, jot your ideas down, work through the questions and exercises honestly, and spend some time thinking about how you'll apply each step to your own life.

One more thing: I encourage you to turn the page ready to explore and discover who you are and how you approach things. Be curious. Be willing to learn. Be willing to suck at some things. And be willing to stretch yourself at every step in the pursuit of self-discovery. Remember—there's no right or wrong here . . . just useful information and self-knowledge that will undoubtedly make your life run much more smoothly. And what could be better than that?

2

STEP 1: DEFINE YOUR TO DO

Ever heard of The Sparkle Effect? If not, well, please allow me to fill you in. The Sparkle Effect is a student-run program that helps teens foster inclusiveness by ensuring students with disabilities can participate in their high schools' cheering and dance programs. The Sparkle Effect has generated more than one hundred inclusive teams across the country and has been featured on *The Oprah Winfrey Show* and in *People* magazine. The program's founder, Sarah Cronk, has received a ton of awards and recognition, including being named one of the L'Oreal Women of Worth for 2012 and winning the 2011 Do Something Award's grand prize of $100,000.

But when Sarah first got started in 2008, she was a fifteen-year-old student at Pleasant Valley High School in Bettendorf, Iowa, who noticed a problem at her school: students with special needs and disabilities were being excluded from after-school sports and activities. Sure, there were segregated activities and clubs these students could participate in, but there was no great way for them to play or perform side-by-side with their peers, which was all they really wanted. Sarah knew the issue went well beyond the walls of her school, but she realized she couldn't take it all on. Not then, anyway. So she started where she was—a member of the cheering squad—and decided she needed to figure out how cheerleading at her school could work with a policy of inclusion. Her motivation? To positively impact other students and her community.

Sarah realized she was onto something by the end of that year. "I thought just doing it at my school was a big enough deal to me when we first got it going. We only started two teams in that first year, but I saw how much attention it received right away, how popular it got, and I realized we were onto something." And with that, The Sparkle Effect was born.

Though The Sparkle Effect has grown and evolved in the years since it was first conceived, it all started with a simple, clear vision. Knowing what she was trying to create—inclusion in after-school activities at her school—helped Sarah be successful that first year. And the rest, as they say, was history.

The Real Question

The question I have for you, for *anyone* with a goal, is this: what do you want to do?

The question might seem simple enough, and it is, but you'd be surprised at how many people have trouble actually answering it. They're too busy running around like chickens with their heads cut off, frantically trying to get it all done. Yet when you get them to slow down and ask them what it is they're trying to accomplish, most of the time they're not exactly sure. They just know they've got a lot of things to do and they have to go, go, go to do them.

Imagine you're packing for vacation. You've dug your suitcase out of the garage, stuffed your toiletries bag with your essential products, downloaded a couple of books onto your e-reader, and even arranged for a neighbor to check in on your cat. But you've forgotten to do one very important thing—figure out where you want to go for your getaway. Sure, you might be ready to head out the door, but without a final destination in mind, the vacation is going to be a complete and total bust.

The same goes for any To Do. You have to know exactly where you're headed, as well as be crystal clear on what you actually want to do, for any task to be truly doable. That's why the essential first step of my process is to define your To Do. In order to do this, it's important to actually state your goal—write it down or say it out loud—and metaphorically put your stake in the ground. By declaring your goal, you're formalizing it and making it real. You're essentially saying to yourself that your pursuit is something you take seriously and that you're all in.

This declaration should include definitive language: *I am going to _____ in the next year, or I am committing to _____ every day this month, or I will do _____ by the end of the month.*

If we skip this step, we run the risk of having our goals remain in dreamland limbo—*someday* I'm going to hike to the top of Mount Whitney, or I *really want* to become a vegetarian. These are fantastic dreams and desires, but they're lacking the specificity and concreteness required for them to actually become accomplishments. "Someday" has a very different meaning than "by the end of the month."

So name it, say it, and make it real.

When Goals Are Vague

Sometimes defining and declaring a To Do is a simple task. Maybe you want to bake apple pie for dessert or you want to sign up for piano lessons or you want to have a yard sale this weekend to make some money off your old clothes and books. Those are all very straightforward To Dos—the thing you want to do or create is implicit in the goal itself. Once you state it, you're good to move on and bake that pie, sign up for those lessons, or hold that yard sale. However, more often than not, To Dos live in a kind of murky place. I like to call it the Land of Vague.

Now, sometimes being vague is a good thing, like when a friend gets a hideous haircut and asks you how she looks. You can vaguely reply with a comment about how her new cut highlights her eyes or enthusiastically throw the question back to her: "Wow! A new haircut! What do *you* think?"

But of course, there are times when being vague is a bad idea, like when you're giving directions or telling your friend your Starbucks order before she runs off to grab you a latte. Another occasion when vagueness isn't your friend? *Goal setting.*

Yet, despite this, many would-be Doers suffer from overly vague goals. When a goal is too vague, it can't be measured, which means there's no way of knowing when and if you've actually reached it. Working toward vague goals is about as productive as running on a life-sized hamster wheel (although at least in that case you're getting a decent workout).

Here's what I mean by a vague goal:

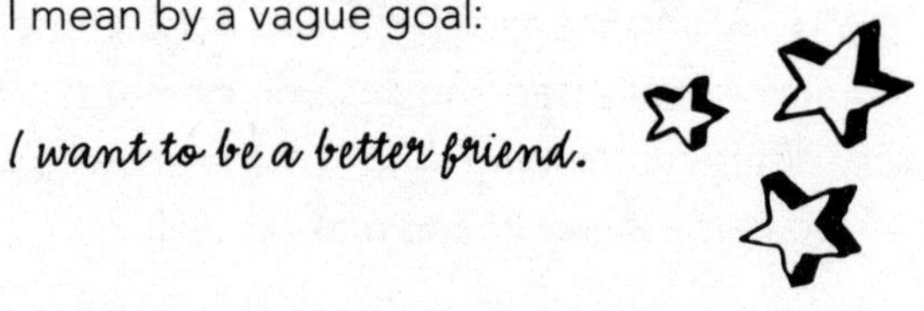

Don't get me wrong—wanting to be a better friend is an excellent pursuit. But what exactly does being a better friend entail? First off, it depends on where you're starting from, as in, what kind of friend are you now? Secondly, it depends on your definition of friendship, which has a lot to do with how you view the world and relationships. What does being a friend mean in relation to your values? Who are you at your core? How do you see the world? Lastly, there's the result: how will you know if you've become a better friend and therefore accomplished what you set out to do?

In order to turn this lovely intention of being a better friend into a doable accomplishment, you'll have to get clear on all those aspects and more so you can rewrite your goal in a way that will allow you to truly cross that baby off your list.

For example, maybe to you being a better friend means not talking behind your friend's back. Or maybe it means planning thoughtful surprises to let your friend know how important she is to you. *Now* you have something to work with, and from there, you can create very clear tasks to tackle—in this case, put a halt to talking behind your friend's back or regularly do something thoughtful for her.

THE DOABLE TEST

To determine if a To Do falls into the too-vague category, ask yourself these three simple questions:

1. Can the goal or the result of the goal be measured or tracked?
2. Are there clear steps I can take to reach my goal or accomplish my To Do?
3. Will I know when I've reached the goal or completed the task?

If you answered no to *any* of these questions, your To Do isn't specific enough yet to pass the Doable test.

If your To Do is vague right now, no sweat. It's normal for some of your goals to be unclear. In fact, many of them start out that way, especially when they spark as concepts or big ideas you feel extra inspired or excited about. All we need to do is shift those ideas into concrete, doable goals by taking a closer look and getting clear on what you will actually be doing.

Here's what I mean:

Vague Goal: I want to be healthier.
Concrete Goals:

- I want to drink eight glasses of water a day.
- I want to exercise four times a week.
- I want to eat at least one serving of whole foods each day.

Vague Goal: I want to be a better student.
Concrete Goals:

- I want to turn in all my homework assignments on time.
- I want to complete all my assigned reading.
- I want to earn a B or higher on all my exams.

A trickier challenge to overcome is when we don't know what completing the task or achieving the goal actually looks like. And that's exactly the kind of information that's crucial when it comes to seeing something through from start to finish. It might seem like a no-brainer that we need to have a clear understanding of the kind of end result we're after, but the reality is, it can sometimes be difficult to figure out, especially when related to vague goals.

Let's say you've set the following goal:

I want to be a good soccer player.

Sounds great! Sure, it's a vague goal, but the associated tasks are seemingly straightforward or, at the very least, could be simple to parse out. The goal of being a good soccer player could easily be made more concrete by getting specific about how exactly you're going to do that. For example, you might decide you're going to practice soccer drills three times a day, cross-train over the weekends, or read books to learn new soccer strategies.

See the difference? Now you've got concrete To Dos to tackle.

But answer me this: How exactly will you know when you've reached your goal of being a good soccer player? In other words, what does being a good soccer player mean? It's not like someone's going to show up on your doorstep, certificate in hand, and announce the big news that you've finally achieved Good Soccer Player status. No, it's much more personal than that.

The question you would have to answer is this: What does being a good soccer player mean to you? Does it mean you score more consistently? Does it mean you've mastered the arts of juggling, dribbling, passing, receiving, and shooting? Does it mean you have enough stamina to get through an entire game without tiring?

These are all results that, with hard work and dedication, can be achieved. And once you've picked the results that resonate with you, you'll have a clear sense of what achieving your goal will look and feel like. In essence, you've made your goal more doable. (I'll talk more about this notion of success and understanding what achieving it looks like in chapter 6.)

Your Terms, Your Control

In order for a goal to be truly doable, achieving it has to be something that's totally within your control. Now, I'm not advocating that you become a control freak. For the record, I am generally of the mind-set that in most situations there is actually very little we can control, save for the way we think and feel. However, when it comes to goal setting and pursuing To Dos, control plays a crucial role.

Why? Because, unless you've mastered the art of the Jedi mind trick, you can't control what anyone else thinks, says, or does. No matter how charming or charismatic or persuasive or fabulous you may be (and I have no doubt that you're all these things and more!), every person is in charge of his or her feelings, thoughts, and actions. Therefore, putting your fate in the hands of others—letting your success be made or broken by another person or group of people—will send you down a road of frustration and into a state of unfulfilled flux. I believe the technical term for this is *meh*. So take this guideline to heart: for a goal to be truly doable, it has to be something you can have 100 percent control over pursuing and achieving.

Let's take the previous example: *I want to be a good soccer player.*

I broke down some associated, concrete tasks (practice soccer drills, cross-train, read soccer books) you can do while getting clear on what you want to ultimately achieve. And all the tasks led to results that were more or less in your control:

- Scoring more consistently

- Being an expert juggler, dribbler, passer, receiver, and/or shooter

- Having enough stamina to last an entire game

But there are also many other potential results you could work toward, such as:

- Making the varsity team

- Being named player of the year

- Getting a full-ride athletic scholarship to your dream school

While the above are great aspirations, and certainly worth working toward, the results aren't totally within your control. There are outside factors that impact whether or not you can achieve them, like coaches, referees, college recruiters, and other teammates. Who knows—you might have the next Hope Solo as a teammate and lose the spotlight to her, or the college recruiter who's been eyeing you all season could retire before offering you a scholarship.

Let's be clear: I'm not suggesting you ditch your big, awesome goals and dreams! On the contrary . . . bring 'em on! The bigger, the better! Just be sure that reaching those goals is something you can own and control.

The Big Why

Being super clear on exactly what you want to do and figuring out what getting there will look like are important steps in making goals and To Dos achievable, but there's one more piece of the puzzle that isn't on most people's radar when it comes to pursuing things: getting clear on your Why.

Why ask why?

Because *why* is where it's at (IMHO). By thinking about your Why for everything you're hoping to do, you're getting clear on your meaning for doing it. And when you can tap into the meaning behind anything on your plate, you unleash a boundless supply of motivation and inspiration that can be used to propel you forward.

Here's what I'm talking about.

Your Why is your personal reason. Your Why connects any task or To Do with who you are and what you're all about. Your Why is an individual thing. It's emotional, it's personal, and it can be incredibly powerful.

For example, say you want to beat your record in the 3000-meter race in track and field next spring. As long as you know your previous record that you want to blow past, you're looking at a very straightforward goal. You know exactly what you're trying to do (beat your previous best time), exactly what you need to do to get there (train, do speed workouts, eat well, be rested for your meets), and you'll obviously know exactly when you've accomplished it (you'll have clocked a race faster than your previous record). Perfect.

But while having that straightforward goal is fantastic as is, let's add in the extra element of a Why and see how it might change things.

Maybe your Why is to qualify for the district, state, or even national competition. Maybe your Why is to get the attention of the track coach of your dream school. Or maybe your Why is proving to yourself that you are capable of doing more than you believed possible. Maybe it's all three.

Now you've defined the concrete goal you want to reach, and you've also honed in on your internal motivation, something that can keep you focused, inspired, and moving forward with strength and determination. All that's left to do is lace up those running shoes and cue the theme song to *Rocky*.

This isn't just a nice, feel-good sentiment either—it's brain science. Simon Sinek, a researcher, TED speaker, and author of the book *Start with Why: How Great Leaders Inspire Everyone to Take Action*, talks about the role your emotional brain—otherwise known as the limbic system—plays in helping you tap into your personal Why. This limbic system is the part of your brain that drives you, not to mention others, to take action. Activate your emotional brain in a positive way, and you'll have an immediate edge in your goal pursuing.

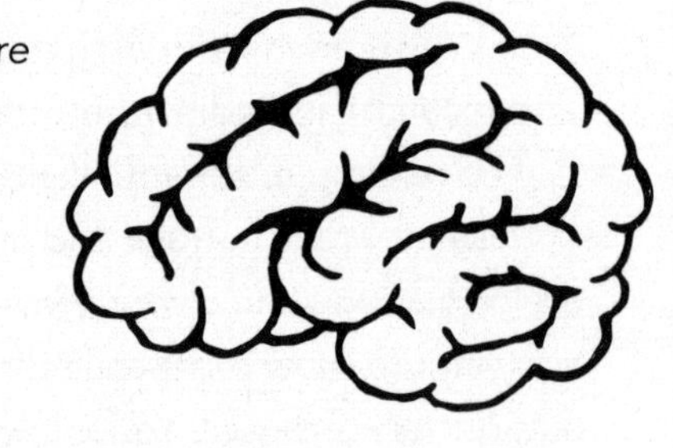

For Grace Li, the idea of a personal Why was not only a driving force but something she couldn't ignore. When an 8.0 magnitude earthquake struck Sichuan, China, in 2008, Grace felt she just had to do *something*. Both her parents were born and raised in China, and the tragedy there struck a deep chord with her. She approached the Red Cross to find a way to get involved, but they initially told her they didn't need much help from twelve-year-olds.

"I thought, regardless of that, I had to do something. I couldn't just stand by and let something like this happen. I wasn't thinking about starting my own nonprofit organization. I thought, *I'll just raise the money by myself.* I just felt like I could still do something on my own," Grace explains.

And did she ever. Grace, along with her younger siblings, Sharon and Eric, raised more than $6,000 that summer, mostly by going door to door. She eventually partnered with her local Red Cross, and together they made sure the money reached children and families impacted by the tragedy in Sichuan. And like Sarah Cronk's The Sparkle Effect, what started as a small, homegrown effort has since turned into a global movement. Grace and her siblings' work has evolved into We Care Act, a nonprofit that engages other young people to help children around the world recover from disasters. Talk with Grace, and you'll hear her powerful conviction behind what she wanted to do. She believed she could make a difference and so she did. Her personal Why actually fueled her toward success.

Cammy Nelson is a recent college graduate and pretty much an all-around kickass girl. She has spoken around the country to share a message of empowerment for girls, has been featured in *CosmoGIRL* as a Project 2024 Girl, founded a nonprofit called Rep Your School—Build a School while she was a student at the University of Wisconsin at River Falls, and was the recipient of the Chancellor's Award for Excellence in Leadership in 2012. Wow! Cammy says her personal Why is behind *everything* she successfully works toward.

"For me, in terms of getting clear on goal setting, it's about that why—why does this need to happen, and what is it that makes this something I'm passionate about? A lot of what I've done in the past and what I'm really proud of has come from things I feel a lot of passion toward," Cammy explains.

She describes how this passion helped her be clear about what she wanted to create through her organization Rep a School—Build a School. "I was sitting in the university commons at my school watching people come down the stairs for dinner, and for some reason, there seemed to be a lot of people wearing our university apparel that evening. As I was sitting there looking at it, I thought, *Why can't some of the money that goes toward buying these clothes be used to do something good?*"

Cammy says the definition of *something good*—which ended up being the idea of building a school—came later. "That's when it felt right and I got excited about the idea that we can get access to education for kids all around the world." Her organization took a portion of proceeds from university apparel and used it to help build a school in an underdeveloped nation. "So my clarity came from the passion that I have for education in addition to the passion I had for making a difference through small acts like buying a T-shirt."

Why Not

From Grace and Cammy's stories, it's easy to understand how your personal Why can actually become part of your recipe for success. Most of the time, that is. The rest of the time? Exploring your Why might make you realize your goal isn't actually something you even want to do. Useful info to have, don't you think?

Say your goal is to land a lead in the class play. You've identified the three possible parts you're after, prepped an awesome audition monologue, and cleared your schedule for the tryouts. Yet, when you ask yourself *why* you want to be cast in a leading role, you realize your primary reason is because you don't want to disappoint your mom. After all, she thinks you're a natural-born actor, and you want her to be proud of you. When you dig deeper, you might also discover you don't really have any skin in the game and that when it comes right down to it, you'd much rather help build the props and set than be in the spotlight. On top of everything else, you were hoping to work extra hours at your part-time job to save up for a Tory Burch bag, and spending every night at rehearsals doesn't really fit into your plan.

By just asking the simple question—why?—you can see that this goal of being a lead in the play probably isn't one worth pursuing. Because at the end of the day, it's not actually something you want to achieve.

And I guarantee you this—if you begin working toward a goal that you don't truly want to achieve and that you're not fully committed to accomplishing, the chances of reaching it are slim to none. For a goal or a To Do to be doable, it actually has to be something you want to do . . . and for a reason that's meaningful to you.

THE WHY TEST

The quick and easy way of figuring out if a goal should be cut from the bucket list is to see if it passes the Why Test. Ask yourself if your Why is rooted in a fear of:

- **Disappointing someone else:** Are you concerned that if you don't do something, you will let someone else—a friend, a sibling, a parent, a teacher, a coach—down? Does your concern over disappointing another person outweigh your own personal desires associated with the To Do?

- **Missing out:** Fear of missing out (FOMO) is a very real thing and it's been behind many an ill-fated pursuit. Doing something because you're afraid that by not doing it you'll be forgotten or perceived as less important or worthy is a recipe for disaster. Plus, it just feels crappy.

- **Others judging you:** Do you worry about what others will think of you to the point that you embark on endeavors in the hopes of controlling others' perceptions?

If you answered yes to any of these, then consider dropping this goal like a hot potato. Or at the very least, explore whether or not you can reset your intention to make the goal meaningful to *you*.

Remember this truth: the only person whose thoughts you can control is you. People will think what they think. Your Why trumps another person's—at least when it comes to your *own* things—any day of the week.

Essentially, if your Why is tied to fear of any kind, it's an indicator that you're more focused on others' thoughts and feelings about you than on what *you* really want. And that, frankly, is pretty darned disheartening. That's not to say you can't or won't complete your To Dos if your Why is outwardly focused, but being fueled by fear of how others might judge you instead of openness, curiosity, and enthusiasm can absolutely make it more of a struggle.

And even if our Whys aren't rooted in fear or concern over disappointing someone, sometimes further exploration can show us that our intentions behind what we're doing are misplaced. Sometimes we're following stories for our lives that someone else is writing.

It's Up to You

Sahar Osmani, president of the San Diego State University chapter of Coaching Corps, was five years old when she uttered the words, "I'm going to be a lawyer when I grow up!" much to her parents' amusement. From that day on, Sahar had it embedded in her mind that she would be a lawyer someday. That notion became part of her unquestioned personal story all the way through high school graduation. But when she got to college and started taking political science and other prelaw classes, she had an aha moment and realized that what she was doing wasn't actually what she was passionate about at all.

Sahar explains, "I had to look back at my goals and answer those questions: What do I want to do with my life? What do I want to accomplish? What am I attached to? What things do I like? So that's how I ended up defining what I really wanted. And finding a purpose in my education and in what I wanted to do with my life."

As it turns out, Sahar is passionate about working in intel, or special investigations. So she switched her focus at school, became a member of the Air Force ROTC, and is taking the steps she needs to take to make her dream and plan a reality. Now that her personal passion and Why are in alignment with her goals, I have no doubt she'll be unstoppable.

STEP 1 SUMMARY

Congratulations! If you've read through this chapter, you're on your way to making anything doable. Taking this first step gives you a solid foundation for consciously pursuing whatever is on your plate. Here is a recap of the key points:

Step 1: Define Your To Do: By defining your To Do, you clarify not only what you want to do but why you want to do it. To do this:

- **Declare what it is you want to achieve, either verbally or in writing.** For example, *I want to bake an apple pie or I want to sign up for piano lessons or I want to have a yard sale this weekend.*

- **Turn vague goals into concrete goals.** Can the goal or the result of the goal be measured or tracked? If not, adapt the goal so you can answer that question with a definitive yes. *I want to be healthier* becomes *I want to eat at least one serving of whole foods each day. I want to be a better student* becomes *I want to turn in all my homework assignments on time.*

- **Explore what completing the goal itself will look and feel like.** How exactly will you know when you've become a good soccer player? Will you score more consistently? Will you have mastered the arts of juggling, dribbling, passing, receiving, and shooting?

- **Make sure completing the To Do is within your control.** *I want to get a full ride to college on a soccer scholarship* depends on other people choosing you, but *I want to raise my stamina so I can get through an entire game without tiring* is all on you.

- **Uncover your personal Why for pursuing the To Do, and make sure it's personal and meaningful.** For example, *I want to prove to myself that I'm capable of doing more than I believed possible.*

3

STEP 2: DETAIL THE LITTLE TASKS

What does it take to win the prestigious Google Science Fair, an online science competition sponsored by Google, Lego, and *National Geographic* and *Scientific American* magazines, among others? For Naomi Shah, winner of the 2011 award in the fifteen-to-sixteen age category, it took a lot of passion, time, and organization, not to mention the willingness to move forward on her sometimes painstakingly slow research, one step at a time.

"In school, you're given these assignments where people tell you the timeline and the timeframe that you're supposed to finish them in. So you get like a worksheet in math and then the next day you have to come in with it completed. But in my own research, I didn't work with a mentor. So I didn't have someone say, 'By Monday, I need you to have these articles read, and by next Monday, I need you to learn how to use X or Y equipment.'

"I had to kind of set those smaller goals for myself," Naomi explains. "My research is one of the biggest parts of my life. I have school, and I really try to do well in school. I take advanced classes because I'm really interested in science and math. But then outside of school, I hang out with my friends. I'm a swimmer. And then I focus a lot of my time on my research.

"In order to make sure I don't waste the time that I'm focusing on my research, I've learned to break it up into chunks so I can better fulfill whatever goal I'm trying to accomplish. So at the end of the day, my goal isn't to come up with some type of breakthrough with my research. It's to do a very small portion of it. It could be that at the end of the day, I'll understand an article I've read. Or at the end of the day, I'll have run two different trials in my experiment.

"I think writing out how I see myself progressing through a project and then working on it like that has really helped me. I think that's going to help me in college too, where the professors aren't going to be sitting on my head saying, 'You know, you have to get this project done.' Instead it's going to be me mapping out my time into little chunks."

Get Tiny

Naomi has gotten really good at step 2 of the Doable process: Detailing the Little Tasks. So good, in fact, that she is able to find time to make regular progress on her breakthrough research about how air quality affects lung health, particularly for people with asthma (hence the Google Science Fair win!).

While we started the Doable process by getting absolutely clear about what we're trying to do, step 2 is about getting *tactical*. It's about taking that clarity of vision and zooming in with a microscope. So when I say "detail the little tasks," I'm talking minuscule. Literally, each and every tiny task associated with accomplishing the bigger-picture goal.

Because no matter how badly you want to reach the goal, how clear you are on your Why for wanting to get there, and how specific you are about what the outcome should be, without taking the time to figure out the individual tasks to get there, you'll be hard-pressed to cross the finish line.

When I was researching this book, I asked a slew of teens to tell me what prevented them from making progress on, let alone completing, all the small, medium, and big things they wanted to get done. One of the most common answers, no matter the size of the task, was a feeling I call *overwhelm.* Many teens said they just didn't know how to get started, and therefore, they never began. As a result, their goals—whether lofty and inspired or practical and straightforward—remained these elusive, just-out-of-reach desires. On top of that, their inability to follow through and accomplish what they set out to do left them feeling guilty and frustrated. And it probably goes without saying that guilt and frustration aren't the best ingredients for productivity.

The good news is, these teens aren't alone—not knowing where to start is a common struggle for many would-be Doers. And the bigger the goal, the more overwhelm comes into play. In fact, big, hairy goals can lead to a twist on analysis paralysis—that condition where over-thinking leads to so much anxiety or uncertainty that a person stays completely stuck. But instead of overanalyzing, in this case, we're *underanalyzing*. The big To Do is composed of so many unknowns that it becomes this mythical destination, unicorns and all, instead of a tangible, let's-get-cracking-and-cross-this-baby-off-the-list kind of pursuit.

But just so we're on the same page here, detailing the little tasks doesn't only apply to big To Dos. Even the smallest, seemingly most doable tasks can become *more* achievable by breaking them down into small chunks. Then, like following a recipe for your favorite baked treat, you mix the ingredients one by one. Do this, and when you're finished, you'll have something to show for it.

This is a strategy Sarah Cronk of The Sparkle Effect uses in her everyday, crazily busy life juggling being a college student with being president of a nonprofit, not to mention everything else she crams into each day. Rather than panic (which would be the obvious and easy choice), Sarah focuses on small tasks.

"I know I'm going to start feeling better if I just pick one thing. Sometimes I just have to stop and do something as small as make my bed, wash a dish, go to the gym, or take a shower. At least it's still productive and it's getting me working toward something. It's very important to focus on those little things until, by end of the day, I finish my To Do list," Sarah explains.

BREAK IT DOWN, BABY

Sarah breaks down everything on her plate into smaller tasks as a way to get through her extensive daily list of To Dos. But this strategy is especially effective when applied to a specific goal. Here's an example to demonstrate what it looks like, step by step.

Say Jessica has wanted to repaint her room for the past year. She detests the soft pink color of the walls. It's so sixth grade—so not who she is now as a teenager and an artist with an edgy aesthetic.

Her parents are cool with her changing the color, but only on the condition that it's 100 percent her deal. The way they see it, they've already painted her room twice, once when she was a baby and once when she was in middle school. "The pink is fine, and the paint is still in great shape. You'll be leaving for college in two years anyway. Can't you just live with it or cover it with posters?"

Sure, she could just make do, but she doesn't want to. She wants her bedroom to be a room she loves and wants to spend time in. And she's got the first Doable step, Defining Your To Do, covered. She knows:

1. What she wants to accomplish (painting her room blue)

2. How she'll know she's completed her task (her room will be blue)

3. Why she wants to do it (to reflect who she is as an artist)

Jessica's even picked out the perfect color—Benjamin Moore's #1638: Midnight Blue. Yet, though she's had the paint swatch pinned above her desk since last year, that's as far as she's gotten. Going from the desire to have a blue room to actually making it happen just feels too hard. She's never painted a room before and doesn't know what's involved, how much it will cost, or how long it will take. The result of these unknowns swirling around in her mind is a lack of action . . . of any kind. And so her room remains a color that is disconnected from the young woman Jessica has become.

Jessica needs to Detail the Little Tasks—break down absolutely everything that has to happen in order for her to move from point A (dissatisfied with her room color and desperate to paint it) to point B (happy and content with her repainted room).

At first glance, the tasks might seem pretty straightforward:

1. Pick a paint color.

2. Buy the paint.

3. Paint the room.

Boom. Mission accomplished, right?

Not necessarily. Though Jessica already has a paint color in mind, there's a reason that's as far as she's gotten. Namely, she doesn't know all the details involved for the next two tasks. On top of that, she doesn't know what she doesn't know—the tasks that are actually missing from the above list.

Because she has no experience painting rooms, the first thing Jessica needs to do is *research*. I'm not talking term paper–level research that would earn Jessica a PhD in interior design, but rather, a cursory look at what she needs to do if she's going to see this thing through.

Luckily, getting information these days is as simple as tweeting a question, looking at Pinterest boards, or posting something on Facebook. And then there's Google. When Jessica searches for the phrase "how to paint an interior room," the search engine spits out more than 50 million results in less than a second, the first one being a step-by-step breakdown of everything a painter needs to know, courtesy of Lowe's home improvement store.

So now that Jessica knows what painting a room entails, she can connect the dots by writing out absolutely everything she needs to do in order to achieve her goal. And when I say "everything," I mean *everything*. Here's what her list might look like:

1. Pick a paint color (already completed).

2. Google Benjamin Moore paints and find out what stores sell it in my town.

3. Measure the height and width of each wall to figure out the total square footage of the surface I need to paint.

4. Call the store to find out how much paint I need to buy and ask how much it will cost.

5. Google instructions for how to paint a room; talk to Jeff's older brother (a contractor) and ask him for some tips.

6. Make a list of the painting supplies I need to buy (rollers, painter's tape, brush, sand paper, and so on).

7. Ask my parents what paint supplies we already have that I can use. For anything I need that we don't have, ask Jeff's brother if I can borrow from him.

8. Gather supplies.

9. Make sure I have enough money to pay for the paint.

10. Figure out how to get the rest of the money if it costs more than I have. (Borrow from mom and dad? Do extra chores? Wait until after my birthday, when I know I'll get money from Grandma?)

11. Once I have all the money, go to the store and buy the paint.

12. Take my posters and other decorations off the walls.

13. Move all my furniture to the middle of the room.

14. Cover my furniture with some sheets (no paint splatter!).

15. Lightly sand the walls.

16. Wipe off the walls with a damp sponge.

17. Use painter's tape along the window frame to protect it from the new paint color.

18. Get some old newspaper and put it on the floor up against the wall.

19. Change into an old T-shirt and my ratty sweats.

20. Make sure I have a damp cloth on hand (to wipe up any spills or splatters).

21. Ask Malika if she wants to come over and help. (?)

22. Put the paint can on some newspaper.

23. Open the can and stir the paint.

24. Pour some paint into the paint tray.

PRODUCTIVITY

25. Dip the roller in and start painting. (!)

26. When done with the main part of the walls, touch up the edges with the paintbrush.

27. Put the lid on the paint can and wash out the brushes.

28. Clean up all the newspaper.

29. Let paint dry (2 hours!).

30. Take the tape off from around my window frame.

31. Move all my furniture back.

32. Woohoo! Room is painted!!

Now that her list is done, it's a good idea for Jessica to go back through it and see if any of the smaller tasks still feel big or icky. If they do, they have a good chance of being hang-up spots that might thwart her well-laid plans. If she finds any, the solution is to break them down even more. For example, Jessica's thirty-first step is "Move all my furniture back." But if that prospect is overwhelming to her, she could actually break it down into even *smaller* tasks:

- Ask my brother if he'll help me move furniture.
- Make arrangements for him to help me before he goes to his part-time job.

- Dust off furniture before moving it back into my awesome new room!

Now, you may think this list is *way* too detailed, and it's true, *every little thing* is broken down into such tiny tasks that many of them could be completed in no time at all and with very little effort. But trust me—getting detailed is worth it. Every time. Why?

Because we are fool-proofing our plan. By detailing each and every task, we shift our mind-set from "overwhelm" to "easy breezy." And this goes for absolutely *every* To Do—even biggies like applying to colleges, writing a novel, or organizing the homecoming pep rally. No matter the task, we can simplify it when we eliminate the mystery and chunk it out into little, doable tasks. Then we move forward, one task at a time.

But what about huge dreams, you ask? Does this strategy apply to big, hairy, audacious goals like starting your own global nonprofit or getting a four-year degree in environmental science?

Absolutely.

Again—it's all about breaking it down. With these huge, long-term dreams, I recommend chunking them down into smaller goals and then treating each of these goals the way you would any other To Do. In my book *In Their Shoes*, I refer to these smaller goals as supporting goals, because they support the main goal, whatever it may be.

For example, if your goal is to get a four-year degree in environmental science and you're a sophomore in high school, breaking this goal into mini-tasks would likely create a To Do list so long it would fill a notebook. Plus, you may not even know what all the important steps are yet.

So you can put together a list of supporting goals—things that you know you'll need to do that you can actually tackle now—and apply the Doable process to each one. In the above example, your supporting goals might include graduating from high school with a transcript that includes the right prerequisites and a solid GPA, identifying and applying to schools with good environmental science programs, and so on.

MIND MAPPING

In the room-painting example, Jessica listed all her mini-tasks, but if you're not a list girl, no problem. There are other ways to explore the tasks you need to do to reach your goals. My favorite? Mind mapping. A mind map is basically a visual, nonlinear way of brainstorming and organizing information that allows you to capture ideas playfully and creatively. The only rule is that there are no rules. You can create mind maps on paper or on the computer, and if you want to get fancy and fun, you can use different-colored pens or markers, draw doodles, break out the BeDazzler . . . get as creative as you want. Here's what a mind map of Jessica's quest for a blue room might look like:

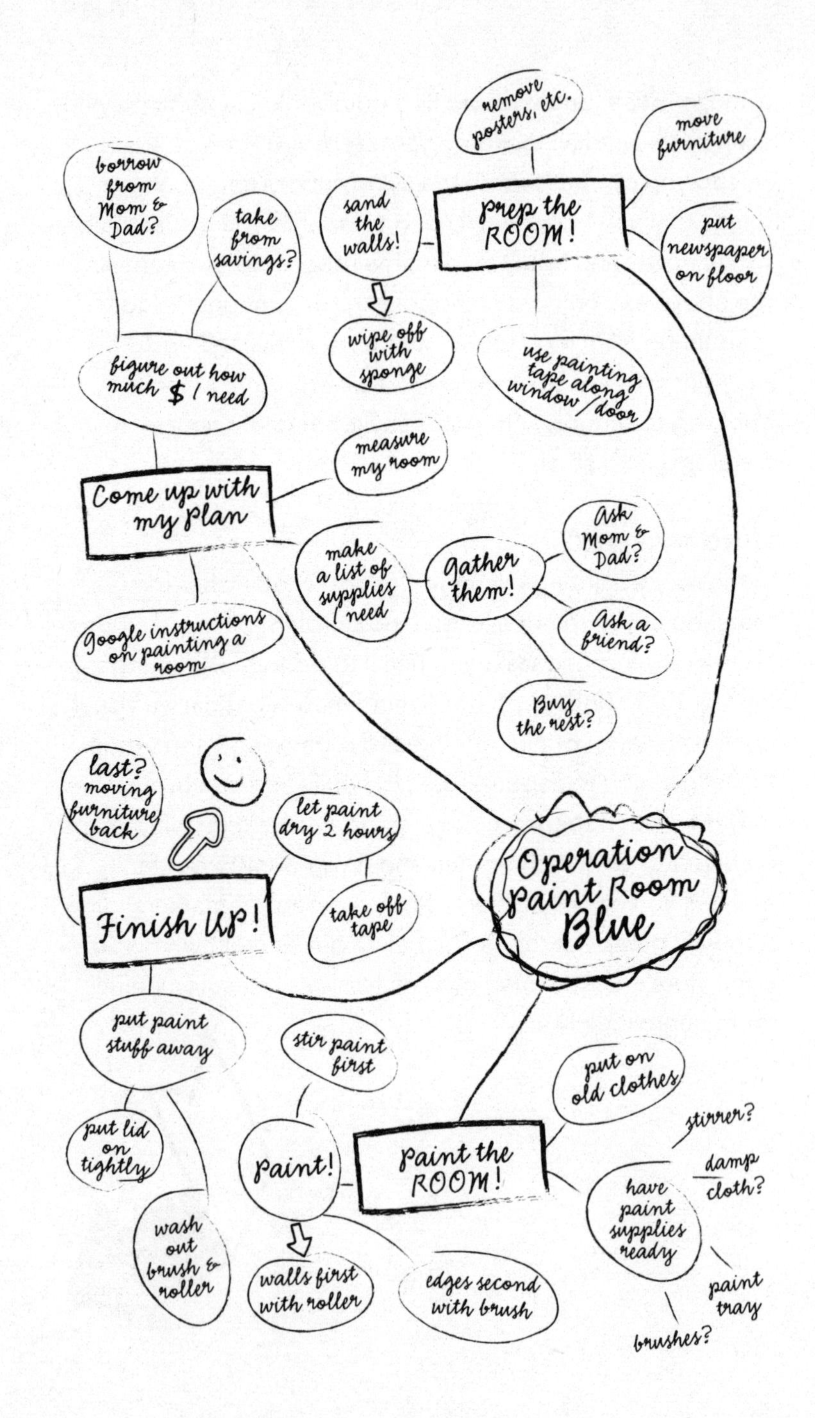
Operation paint Room Blue
Come up with my Plan
figure out how much $ I need
borrow from Mom & Dad?
take from savings?
measure my room
make a list of supplies I need
Gather them!
Ask Mom & Dad?
Ask a friend?
Buy the rest?
Google instructions on painting a room
prep the ROOM!
remove posters, etc.
move furniture
put newspaper on floor
sand the walls!
wipe off with sponge
use painting tape along window / door
Paint the ROOM!
put on old clothes
have paint supplies ready
stirrer?
damp cloth?
paint tray
brushes?
stir paint first
paint!
walls first with roller
edges second with brush
Finish UP!
let paint dry 2 hours
take off tape
last? moving furniture back
put paint stuff away
put lid on tightly
wash out brush & roller

I'm not exactly sure what it is about mind mapping that works so well—plotting and planning in this way just seems to tap into a part of the brain that results in more creative solutions and outside-the-box thinking.

MAP IT!

Give mind mapping a try the next time you want to break down a big To Do. I have a hunch you'll be an instant fan. All you have to do is:

1. Flip open your journal to a blank page.
2. Write down the big goal in large letters in the center of the paper.
3. In smaller writing around the big goal, brainstorm the tasks you need to do in order to reach the primary goal. Draw a box around these main tasks and connect each one to your goal with a line.
4. In even smaller writing, brainstorm the tiny tasks you need to take in order to complete each main task. Circle these small tasks and connect each one with a line to the main task it corresponds with.
5. Color, doodle, and embellish as you like!

Getting Specific by Adding Deadlines

DEADLINES

Now that you've taken the time to write out all the tasks that lead to reaching your goal, you are armed with the information you need to get from dream to reality. *Excellent.*

But what if you're up against a hard-and-fast deadline, or you're one of those people who works better when time factors are at play?

Simple. Go back to your breakdown of tasks and add target dates—dates you either plan to do the task on or dates you hope to accomplish the task by. The important thing here is to always start with the final goal and *work your way backward*—that way you'll always be conscious of the drop-dead date. As you plot out your breakdown, it's important to be super realistic about how long each task might take. If you can, add a little padding to your timeline—if you think something might take you two hours, go ahead and schedule four. This padding prevents you from missing target dates, something that can cause your entire plan to fall apart like a house of cards.

For example, say Tamyra has been struggling with filling out her common application for college. She created a mind map to capture all the big and small tasks she needs to do in order to complete her application. But the final deadline is looming, and because she's prone to procrastination, Tamyra is appropriately concerned she may put off starting that first task for so long that she'll run out of time to do a decent job with it. Still, the pressure's on—she knows a good application is a critical component to gaining acceptance at Skidmore College, her dream school.

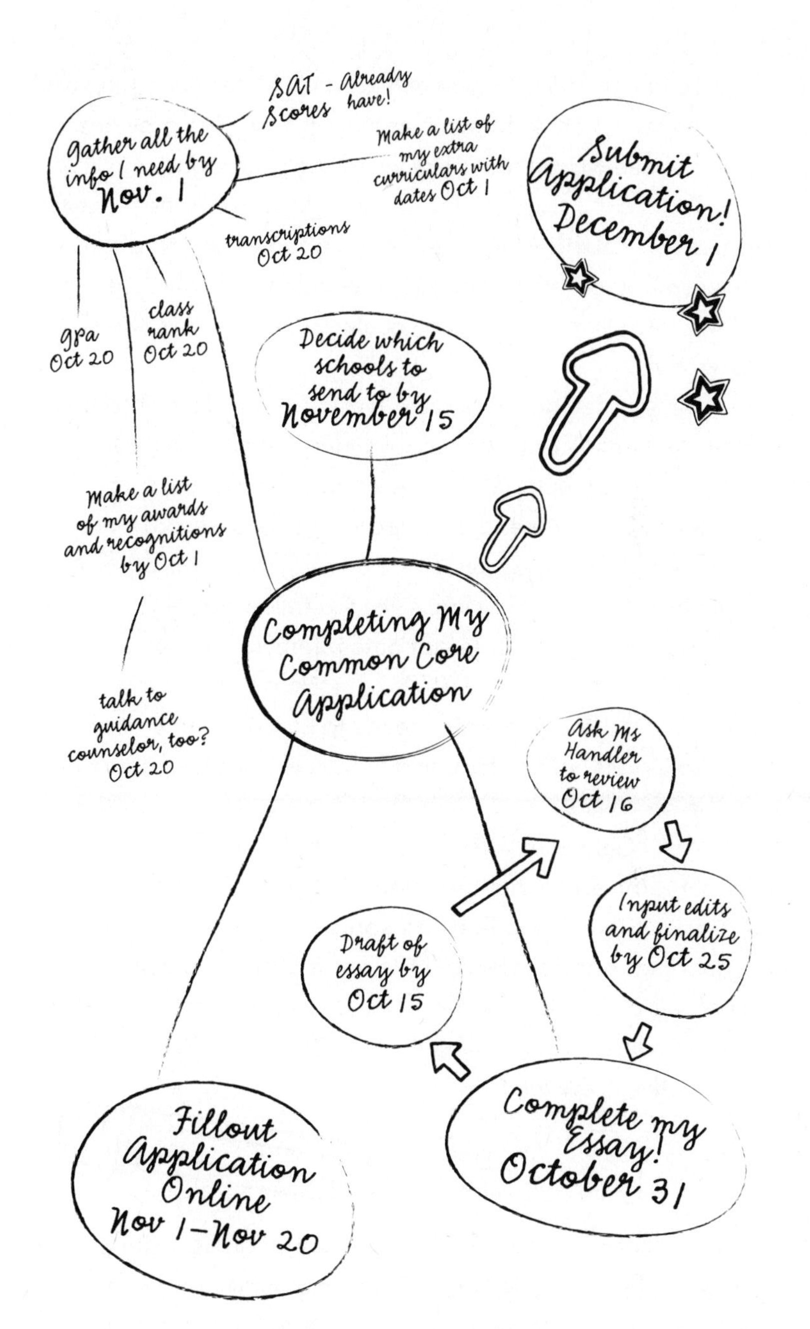
SAT Scores - Already have!
Gather all the info I need by Nov. 1
Make a list of my extra curriculars with dates Oct 1
Submit Application! December 1
transcriptions Oct 20
gpa Oct 20
class rank Oct 20
Decide which schools to send to by November 15
Make a list of my awards and recognitions by Oct 1
Completing My Common Core Application
talk to guidance counselor, too? Oct 20
Ask Ms Handler to review Oct 16
Input edits and finalize by Oct 25
Draft of essay by Oct 15
Fillout Application Online Nov 1–Nov 20
Complete my Essay! October 31

To get specific, Tamyra can go back to her mind map and plug in target dates for each and every task. See previous page to see what it looks like when she's through.

To take it a step further, Tamyra can transfer those target dates to a calendar, whether on her phone, her computer, or even a good ol' fashioned paper calendar. If she uses an electronic calendar, she can set alarms on the days she has tasks due.

Tamyra decides to transfer her tasks and dates into the day planner she uses for school. Since she already looks at her planner multiple times each day to keep track of homework assignments and upcoming tests, she knows she won't miss any target dates for her common application. Now she has something that looks like the following page.

By plugging in her target dates, Tamyra has a clear picture of not only the How and the What but also the When for each and every task she needs to complete to cross her big To Do off her list once and for all (and not lose her mind in the process!).

Anna Gallagher, a freshman at the University of Washington and a member of the prestigious Honors Program there, takes Tamyra's approach one step further. Chuckling, Anna explains, "I like my lists. I have my planner, and I will put important dates in the calendar section, but then I also outline my days, sometimes by the hour." Yes, that's right folks . . . *by the hour.*

Planning to Plan

When it comes to tackling big To Dos and goals, setting aside time to plan is crucial, but is something many people often skip. These people might believe time spent doing anything

School Planner: Week of October 15

Subject	Monday 10/15	Tuesday 10/16	Wednesday 10/17
English	Work on outline for persuasive essay	Finish Outline	Begin draft of essay
AP Biology		Finish researching for my experiment	LAB class—bring in equipment
Russian History	Read Chapter 14 of Russia's War: A History of Soviet Efforts	Chapter 15	Chapter 16
Trigonometry	Homework, pg 79	Homework pages 82–83	Quiz!!
Spanish	Verb vocabulary		Conjugation worksheet
Extracurricular		Yearbook Club after school	
Other Tasks	Complete draft of Common App essay	Ask Ms. Handler to review my essay (for return by Oct 25)	

Subject	Thursday 10/18	Friday 10/19	Saturday/Sunday 10/20–10/21
English	Work on draft	Rough draft due	
AP Biology	In-class experiment day	In-class experiment day	
Russian History	Chapter 17	Chapters 18–20 (by Monday)	
Trigonometry	Homework pages 90–93	No homework	
Spanish	Review chapter and prep for test	Test (covering new verb conjugation)	
Extracurricular		Harvest Dance-7pm	
Other Tasks		Meet with guidance counselor!	Have finished gathering my: GPA, class rank, and transcriptions

other than working on the tasks themselves is time wasted. But that belief couldn't be less true. What these people don't realize is that planning and organizing is *part of the process* of doing anything. In fact, thorough planning can actually speed up the doing part, not to mention make it much less likely that major obstacles will crop up as you put your plan into action. Planning = setting the stage for success.

To make your planning process as simple and fruitful as possible, here are some tips to keep in mind as you apply this strategy to your own goals:

- **Set Aside Time:** When you first name something you want to work toward, give yourself at least a half hour of distraction-free, dedicated time to plot it out—more if it's a big, hairy goal. Time spent planning will almost always save you time down the road.

- **Visualize:** Grab a notebook and pen so you're ready to capture your ideas. Tune out all the noise around you, close your eyes, and imagine yourself actually doing whatever you are trying to do. Visualizing helps you brainstorm possible tasks you may not have thought of otherwise.

- **Do Your Research First:** Researching every little thing you need to do benefits you most when you do it at the *beginning*. Not only do you reduce the possibility of missteps and wasted time, but you can also use what you discover to help you make an informed and organized plan of attack.

- **Understand Who Else Is Involved:** Consider whether other people will have to play roles in accomplishing your To Do. For example, if Jessica needs her dad to take her to the hardware store for painting supplies, she'll want to find out when her dad is available to run that errand. Depending on the goal, some of your tasks may be completely dependent on others' time, input, and/or action. It's good to figure out who these people are up front so you can factor them into your plan.

- **Be Realistic:** Perhaps there is nothing more demotivating than coming up with a plan, getting started, and then realizing your plan is too ambitious to stick to. If you assign deadlines and target dates to the tasks involved in your plan, make sure each task is actually doable in the amount of time you allot. If you aren't sure how much time it will take, err on the side of caution and add more. Worst-case scenario, you'll finish your To Do ahead of schedule.

Like the saying goes, "Better the devil you know than the devil you don't." When you take the time to organize, plan, and prepare, you can move ahead knowing what you're doing, when you want to do it, and how you'll do it. And just like that, you've eliminated guesswork and unnecessary stress throughout your entire Doable journey.

STEP 2 SUMMARY

Acclaimed author and life coach Martha Beck coined the phrase "turtle steps" to refer to the tiny little steps we can take as we move toward any goal. I love this label for the visual reminder it offers and the idea that if we keep moving one small, slow step at a time, we will eventually get where we want to be. When we use this approach, even huge goals, like summiting Mount Kilimanjaro or earning a pilot's license, can be made achievable without the head-spinning sense of overwhelm that often accompanies big dreams.

Step 1: Define Your To Do 

Step 2: Detail the Little Tasks

Take the time to break your To Do down into the smallest possible tasks so you have a clear path for getting from start to finish. And not just for the big goals, either—do it for *every single thing* on your plate. Here are some tips to keep in mind to get the most out of step 2:

- **Chunk your big goal down into small tasks.** This is the number-one antidote to pre-goal-pursuing overwhelm. When you can see all the pieces laid out before you, diving in loses its fear factor.

- **Break your *small* tasks into *tiny* tasks.** Eventually, every action item on your list should be simple, straightforward, and free of the overwhelm ick factor.

If a tiny task still feels overwhelming, find ways to break it down even further.

- **Consider using mind maps as tools to brainstorm smaller tasks for your bigger goal.** The only rule for this nonlinear way of brainstorming and organizing information is that there are no rules. Mind mapping is a great way to tap into your creative problem-solving juju.

- **Take your breakdown of mini-tasks one step further by setting target dates and deadlines for each item.** Start with the final deadline for the completion of your goal and work your way backward, building in padding in case some tasks take longer than you anticipated. Help yourself hit your dates by putting your To Dos and deadlines on your calendar.

- **Take the time to plan, and remember that it's part of the process of doing anything.** To plan effectively: set aside dedicated planning time, visualize what you're trying to do, do your research up front, get clear on what you need from other people, and make sure your timeline is realistic.

4
STEP 3: DEFEND AGAINST OBSTACLES

Lady Gaga, *insecure*? It's hard to believe that word could ever be used to describe the same iconic performer who managed to turn a dress made of meat into a powerful fashion statement.

But flash back to her teen years, and that's exactly how Gaga describes herself. As she said in a 2011 *Rolling Stone* interview, "Being teased for being ugly, having a big nose, being annoying . . . 'Your laugh is funny, you're weird, why do you always sing, why are you so into theater, why do you do your make-up like that?' . . . I used to be called a s--t, be called this, be called that, I didn't even want to go to school sometimes."

Lady Gaga managed to push through her insecurities by staying focused on the big dream—superstardom, a recording contract, fame. But what if she hadn't? What if she had bought into the obnoxious, hurtful things fellow students said about what a "freak" she was? What if she'd given in to her insecurities? Can you imagine a world without Gaga's soulful music, provocative outfits, and anti-bullying Born This Way Foundation?

Obstacles, Obstacles, Everywhere

Everyone has obstacles that can get in the way of achievements. Real or imagined, physical or mental, big or small, these obstacles have the potential to shut down the party before it even gets started. So what's a girl on a mission to do?

Not what you might think. Forget about ignoring your insecurity or fears and plowing ahead on a wing and a prayer. Sooner or later, what's at the root of those fears and insecurities is going to catch up with you and put the kibosh on your big plans.

Your best shot here? *Leaning into the obstacles.* I'm talking about getting to know them like you would a long lost, and slightly annoying, great-aunt. You know . . . the one who shows up on Christmas, presents you with a tacky animal sweater as a gift, and expects to see you wearing it by dinner.

Why? Because the obstacles that get in the way of getting things done are *actually a part of you.* They're born from your thoughts, and they're not necessarily going anywhere. So you might as well get to know them. Befriend them. Kill them with love. It works . . . trust me.

Step 3 of the Doable process is to Defend against Obstacles, the kinds of obstacles anyone on a mission might experience. As you read through this chapter, explore the types of roadblocks you typically face: your own patterns, unhelpful habits and, most important, unhealthy thinking—those thoughts that do nothing more than keep you stuck. Being proactive and coming up with a plan for overcoming the obstacles you're bound to face is your best defense against them.

The Mother of All Obstacles: *Procrastination*

Marni Bates is an author of young adult books who also happens to be a young adult. In fact, she published her first book—an autobiography named *Marni*—at age nineteen. And I should know because, in the spirit of full disclosure here, I edited it. I knew I wanted to include Marni in *Doable* when I started writing it because, after witnessing her write her memoir under tight deadlines, deliver a great manuscript, and be a pro about promoting it, all while balancing the pressures that come with life as a freshman in college, I knew she was pretty amazing at getting stuff done. She must be—at the age of twenty-four, she's written and published five novels in the past four years and has more on deck. But I also know that Marni struggles with the P-word. Yes folks . . . I'm talking about *procrastination*.

PROCRASTINATION

For Marni, procrastination looks like surfing online, doodling, watching videos, or reading other people's books. "Basically, it looks like anything that isn't writing because that's the one thing I'm postponing," she explains.

Marni knows herself well enough to realize she can't actually focus at home when she's writing because she could choose to do so many other things besides write, and there's no one there to call her on it.

"If I'm in a public place with my headphones on, then I know I'm surrounded by other people, and I feel obligated to be doing my work. I've usually spent money on a cup of coffee so I have a monetary investment in getting something out of this time to really make it pay off, and I have a better likelihood of focusing and getting my work done. I have to be willing to give myself some downtime and then to know when to crack the whip, which is really hard. But yeah, I procrastinate."

One thing I know is that Marni's not alone. It would be impossible to write about obstacles to getting things done without tackling the issue of procrastination. Though there are always underlying reasons for procrastination, which we'll explore later in this chapter, this catch-all epidemic of chronically putting things off is probably the number-one excuse for unfinished projects or unreached goals.

Let's get real—most of us procrastinate on some level when it comes to things we're not really into, like emptying the dishwasher, cleaning our bedrooms, or writing that term paper on the Kyoto Protocol. Makes sense, right? When we have something on our plates that doesn't look so great, it's much easier to push it off to the side than to take that first bite. So we delay and we put off and we find *so* many other, much more appealing, things to do instead (like placing decals on our nails or playing with the hamster or watching a *Teen Mom* marathon), planning to get to the above-mentioned task, you know, later. The problem is, for many people, *later* never comes.

WHY WE PROCRASTINATE

But here's the *really* interesting thing: it's not just undesirable To Dos that are thwarted by procrastination. Ask any writer whose unfinished novel, her self-proclaimed passion project, sits in a file on her desktop, neglected, while she spends hours combing through her Facebook newsfeed or juggling a dozen games of Words with Friends.

So, what's the deal? Why do well-intentioned go-getters essentially choose self-sabotage over success? And while we're on the topic, is procrastination a choice after all? Scientists say yes. According to *Psychology Today*, about 20 percent of people are "chronic procrastinators," and not necessarily because of poor planning or time-management skills. The truth is, most procrastinators delay because they're afraid of failing to live up to their standards of perfection.

Whatever the reason, procrastination not only sucks away your time but also keeps you stuck in a spin cycle and can become a habitual way of going through life.

PROCRASTINATION SENSATION

So how about you? Are you a chronic procrastinator? Answer these questions with either "Totally me," "Sometimes me," "Rarely me," or "Never me" to see how many sound like you:

1. When I have a school assignment, I wait until the last minute to get it done (that is, if I manage to get it done at all).

2. If I don't know how to do something perfectly, it's nearly impossible for me to get started.

3. If a task feels overwhelming, I tend to distract myself with other things.

4. I figure I'll reach a point where doing what I have to do will come easily, so I sit around and wait for inspiration to strike.

5. I regularly miss deadlines, whether for things I *have* to do or for things I *want* to do.

If you answered "Totally me" or "Sometimes me" to more than one question, chances are you have some procrastination tendencies that make it challenging for you to tackle your To Dos. But wait . . . there's hope.

PROCRASTINATION EMANCIPATION

Even chronic procrastinators can manage to get things done—take former President Bill Clinton, who was known for his classic procrastination tactics, or painter Leonardo da Vinci, who took sixteen years to finish painting the *Mona Lisa*. (I'm glad he eventually finished his masterpiece, but seriously, who needs an unfinished painting, not to mention a school project or unresolved social dilemma, hanging over her head for more than a decade?)

Procrastination emancipation doesn't necessarily have to do with making fancy schedules or posting reminders all over your desk. And it's not about cutting out all your social time or extracurriculars either. In reality, most procrastinators actually have *plenty* of time to get their To Dos done—being too busy has nothing to do with it. So what's the key to freeing yourself from this not-so-helpful habit?

The answer comes when you ask yourself this simple, little question: why?

As in, *why* do you put things off? *Why* do you regularly miss deadlines? *Why* are you so concerned about doing it perfectly?

One of the most important things life coaches do is ask thought-provoking questions like these to encourage their clients to dig deep and discover new truths about themselves. And while working with a coach is great, you can also uncover the answers on your own by practicing some DIY Coaching. The key is to be brutally honest with yourself and to remember that there are no right or wrong answers. Again, the theme here is *self-knowledge.*

DIY COACHING: YOUR NEW TRUTH

After answering questions about why you do what you do, you can go through a very easy process for developing a new truth about yourself. Don't just answer the questions in your mind, though. Write them down! This is important stuff! Grab your journal or use your Doable workbook (download here: www.debbiereber.com), and jot down your responses to the following questions:

1. Think about the last time you had something you either wanted to do or had to do but struggled to get it done because of procrastination. Write it down.

2. Why do you think you kept putting off the task? Write down as many of the following reasons as apply:

- I didn't have enough information to get started.
- I didn't have enough time to fit it in.
- I didn't have the support I needed.
- I didn't know how to break it down.
- I was afraid of screwing up or blowing it.
- I don't like taking risks.
- I wasn't sure I would be successful.
- I got distracted . . . *a lot.*
- I lost interest.
- I didn't have a strategy for planning and executing the task.
- I got overwhelmed at the thought of starting something new.
- I lost momentum and couldn't get it back.

- I usually don't finish things, so I figured, *Why bother even trying?*

- I didn't believe I had what it took.

- I didn't have the energy to follow through.

- It felt too hard.

- I thought it was too boring.

- I didn't care enough to do it.

3. Now, pick one of the reasons that clicks with you the most as something that regularly stands in your way. Write it down. (For example, *I got distracted.*)

4. When you reflect on this situation, what emotion accompanies the reason you stated? Choose an emotion that resonates for you. Write it down. (For example, *frustration, annoyance, anger, sadness, apathy, confusion, overwhelm, or indifference.*)

5. What thoughts about yourself were going on in your head that resulted in the above emotion? Write down as many as come to your mind. (For example, *I always get distracted. I never finish anything. I'm a big failure because I can't see anything through.*)

6. Now consider how those thoughts probably aren't totally true. What is the *reality* of the situation? Can you come up with an example (or a few) that disproves your crappy thought? (For example, *Okay, I did finish my science project. And I actually turn in most of my homework on time. And if I really think about it, I can find tons of examples of things I actually did see through.*)

7. Since you basically just disproved one of the crappy thoughts that's behind your procrastination, it's time to come up with your *new truth*—a statement that reflects what's actually true in a way that feels positive and optimistic as it propels you forward. Write down your new truth. (For example, *I sometimes get distracted, but I usually finish what I start.*)

Write that new truth where you can see it often. Post it on your wall or your bathroom mirror. *Memorize it.* Because when you are focused on that reality as opposed to thoughts that feel bad and keep you stuck, *that's* when you start to move beyond procrastination. *That's* when things get done.

Did you follow that DIY Coaching process to uncover your new truth? First we figured out the reasons for procrastinating, and then we identified the not-so-great emotions that went along with those reasons. Because our emotions result from our thoughts, we explored those thoughts and realized they were actually crappy thoughts that we can dispute. So we identified what the *reality* was instead of those crappy thoughts, and then we decided to state a new truth that shows our true potential.

Let's take a look at the more common obstacles people face when trying to get stuff done and see how we can apply the idea of DIY Coaching to them for an improved outcome.

Common Obstacles

Procrastination is by far the most common obstacle Doers struggle with, but it's really just a symptom of something bigger going on. Most of those things that get in your way come from your head—your thinking, your fears—*not* your reality. Work on the way you're thinking and you'll notice that you're more able to do your thing. And it gets easier. I promise.

You've just explored some of your own reasons for procrastinating, and more than likely, they boil down to one of the few nearly universal hurdles people face when they're trying to get things done, whether they're looking to change the world or change their sheets. Here's a closer look at not only what might be getting in your way but also how to defend against these obstacles so they don't become barriers to reaching your goals. And it always starts with a deeper look at what's really going on in your head.

OBSTACLE: CRAPPY THINKING

As the previous exercise showed, on some level, almost every obstacle would-be go-getters face boils down to the fact that we're buying into what I like to call crappy thinking. I'm talking about those thoughts going through our heads that are based in fear instead of reality—the kind that make all our insecurities rear their ugly little heads . . . the kind that will stop us dead in our tracks.

Crappy thinking is that inner dialogue that likes to remind us of our greatest screw-ups anytime we start to go outside our comfort zones. It might sound like this: *No one takes you seriously. What were you thinking, trying out for varsity? You're not even close to good enough to make the team.* Or this: *Everyone's going to think you're a loser for getting dumped by him.* Or even this: *Raising your hand is not worth the risk. You'll die of embarrassment if you get it wrong.*

Sound familiar? We each have our own, personal inner critic who has a strong, and warped, opinion about pretty much anything we do outside our safety bubbles.

Defense Strategy: While your inner critic may think she's protecting you (from failure, from fear, from being uncomfortable) by encouraging you to quit while you're ahead, she doesn't actually know what she's talking about. Furthermore, she doesn't get to run your life. You just have to call her on her crap. Here's how:

1. Notice what your inner critic has to say by tuning in to the voice in your head—the one that makes you think twice before doing something you want to do. What kinds of things does she like to remind you of (past failures, current insecurities, future fears)? Keep a list of her greatest hits.

2. Realize that those crappy thoughts going through your mind courtesy of your know-it-all inner critic are nothing

but a bunch of *words*. They're thoughts. They're not true. They're not you.

3. Just as you came up with new truths when you explored your procrastination tendencies, replace these crappy thoughts with new ones. Optimistic ones. Positive ones. Truer ones.

4. Repeat as necessary.

JOURNAL: DIY COACHING—KICKING CRAPPY THOUGHTS

Remember, writing something down makes it even more powerful than saying it or thinking it. Grab your journal or Doable workbook, and let's really kick these crappy thoughts. (We'll be exploring all these obstacles in writing, so keep it handy.) Get down to some DIY Coaching and answer these questions:

1. What kinds of circumstances typically unleash my inner critic? (For example, *Anytime I'm in a new social situation. When I try to do something I've never done before. When I'm working toward a goal others are skeptical of.*)

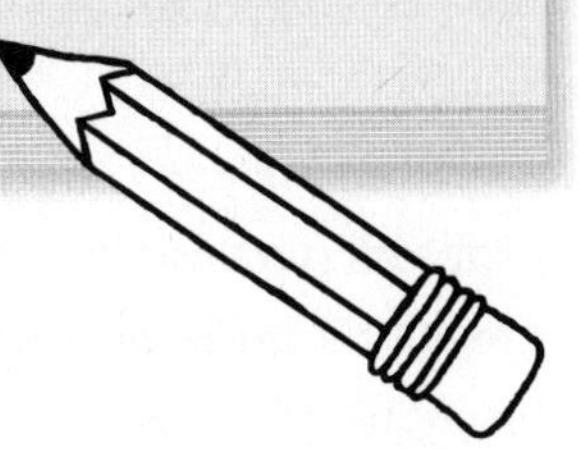

2. What are my inner critic's greatest hits that she repeats anytime I'm working toward a big goal? (For example, *You're going to make a fool of yourself. People will find out you're not that smart. You'll never actually reach your goal, so why bother trying?*)

3. What is the actual truth that these greatest hits don't reflect? (Go through each answer to question 1 and write down what's *really* going on. For example, *In every social situation, I find someone to connect with. No one was born knowing how to do everything. I've reached many goals in the past, and I'm capable of doing it now.*)

4. What greatest hits of my own can I come up with to replace the lame ones played by my inner critic? (Go through each one from question 2 and come up with your new truth. For example, *New social situations can be challenging, but they're almost always worth it. I love learning how to do new things. It's exciting to work toward new goals, and it feels great to accomplish them.*)

Teen fashion blogger Ella Viscardi doesn't have a problem getting things done—she's focused, determined, a quick self-study, and 100 percent committed to her creative projects. She's tackled obstacles before they've even come up, like figuring out the tech side of her site on her own and coming up with a doable schedule for balancing school life with her blogging responsibilities. The one obstacle that she really had to overcome involved her crappy thinking about whether what she did had value in the real world.

"In the beginning, it was challenging because of all the different websites I was looking at. It's hard when you start to compare yourself unrealistically to other people in terms of knowing how successful they've been. I'm only sixteen, not an adult like most of the other bloggers I was looking at," Ella explains.

"I also worried about judgments from other people, like other teenagers at my school if they were to find out I was doing this. I didn't share what I was doing with other people for a while because I didn't know what they'd think."

Luckily, Ella tackled her crappy thoughts head-on and moved past them. To halt the compare-and-despair cycle, she stopped visiting the other sites that were making her feel insecure and turned her focus back to her own writing and doing the things that were important to and for her. Getting over her fear about judgments from her peers took a little more time, but eventually she learned that her passion project was really important to her and was something she put a lot of time into—that it was worth sharing. "That's definitely been a part of my growth. I've gotten positive feedback from friends and other websites, so that's helped me become more confident and want to expand and start to share what I'm doing with more people," she says.

And it seems to have worked well for her. Today, three years after starting her blog, *Ella Etcetera*, she's garnering mainstream attention, including being picked up as a Fashion Click blogger by *Teen Vogue*.

OBSTACLE: OVERWHELM

Overwhelm is an *emotional* state . . . the feeling that there's too much to do, there's too little time, or things are just plain too hard (or maybe all three). But because overwhelm is an emotion, it's not necessarily grounded in fact or reality—it comes from a different part of your brain than the place where logic and reason is stored. Overwhelm looks a lot like stress, and as a result, your body might be responding to a situation similarly to how it would if you had just run into a bear during a summer hike. That's because overwhelm can trigger the fight-or-flight response, which might lead to physical symptoms like insomnia, headaches, nausea, or the jitters. It goes without saying that these conditions don't exactly cheer, "Be happy and productive!"

Defense Strategy: The key to squashing overwhelm is to *get out of your head.* Your big, beautiful brain, the same one that stores oodles of valuable info and enables you to do things like make smart decisions or simplify $7(-3q^2 + 4q)$, is not thinking rationally in this state. Just like scientists believe people's IQ actually drops when they experience anger, rational thinking goes out the window when stress, anxiety, and overwhelm are triggered.

To get out of your head, *stop*, *breathe*, and *think*. (Yes, that is Steve's strategy for dealing with frustration on *Blue's Clues*, but hey, it works here, too.) *Stop*, as in, stop what you're doing, stop moving, stop thinking . . . just *stop*. *Breathe*, as in close your eyes and take ten slow, deep breaths, clearing your mind and focusing only on the air going in and out of your body. *Think*, as in think about what you are feeling most overwhelmed about; think about how to simplify your To Do by breaking it down into tiny, doable tasks; think about how better able you are to do your thing when you're calm, clear, and focused.

When you remind yourself to focus on what's happening in each moment—not tomorrow, not next week, not next month, but *right now*—and you stop your mind from spiraling out of control on an emotional bender, you can keep your overwhelm in check.

JOURNAL: DIY COACHING—OVERCOMING OVERWHELM

1. What is it about my To Do that is making me feel overwhelmed?

2. How do I feel after I close my eyes, relax my body, and take ten slow, deep breaths, turning off my brain as best I can and tuning in to my body?

3. What are five things I can do to help myself get grounded, stop emotional spiraling, and clear my head so I can be in the moment? (For example, *run, listen to music, do yoga, take a nap, or take a shower.*)

4. What reality and new truth can I remind myself of when I start to spiral in the vortex of overwhelm? (For example, *I have time to get everything done,* or *I can take things one moment, one day, and one task at a time.*)

OBSTACLE: DISTRACTION

What else is competing for your attention as you read this page? An incoming text? Music coming from your brother's bedroom? The kajillion other things on your mind, like homework, social drama, deadlines, family stuff, and more? Whatever it is, I have no doubt your attention is being tugged at constantly. As a result, distraction is a very real obstacle when it comes to getting things done—even more than you might realize.

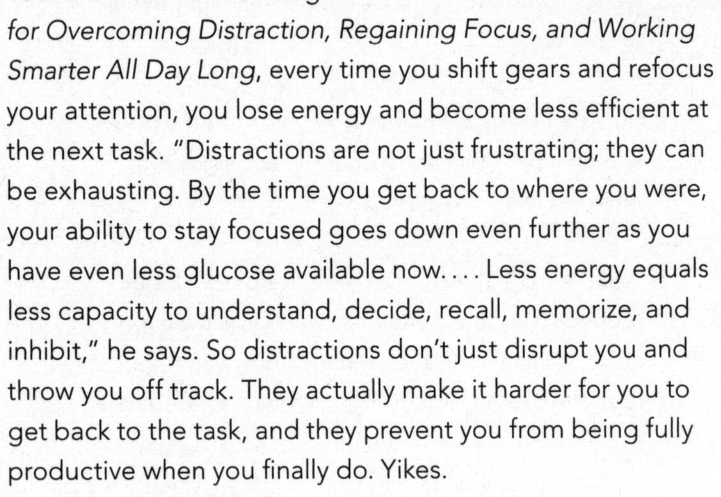

As David Rock describes in his book *Your Brain at Work: Strategies for Overcoming Distraction, Regaining Focus, and Working Smarter All Day Long*, every time you shift gears and refocus your attention, you lose energy and become less efficient at the next task. "Distractions are not just frustrating; they can be exhausting. By the time you get back to where you were, your ability to stay focused goes down even further as you have even less glucose available now. . . . Less energy equals less capacity to understand, decide, recall, memorize, and inhibit," he says. So distractions don't just disrupt you and throw you off track. They actually make it harder for you to get back to the task, and they prevent you from being fully productive when you finally do. Yikes.

Defense Strategy: Combating the obstacle of distraction is a matter of being aware of the things that typically distract you and finding ways to eliminate or minimize those distractions *before* you get to work. If you know you can't resist the pull of your cell phone (even when it's on vibrate), put it in another room, out of sight and earshot, before you begin. If you can't focus in your bedroom or the coffee shop, experiment until you find the venue that works for you. If you're easily distracted by random sounds, try wearing noise-canceling headphones or putting on loud music to help you focus. Get to know your personal distraction reactions and face them head on to create the ideal environment for you to be in the flow.

As I described earlier, author Marni Bates deals with her distraction tendencies by getting out of the house and heading to a coffee shop. Once she's away from her books and has spent some money on coffee, she can focus on what she's trying to get done.

JOURNAL: DIY COACHING—DEFEATING DISTRACTION

1. What kinds of things tend to distract me when I'm trying to focus and work?
2. How can I combat every distraction on my list? (Brainstorm at least one prevention strategy for each distraction you listed in question 1.)
3. In a perfect world, what would my environment for getting things done look like? (Describe it in as much detail as possible.)
4. How and/or where can I create, modify, or find an environment like the one I just described?

OBSTACLE: NOT ENOUGH TIME

You'd think everyone knows there are only twenty-four hours in a day, but apparently some people (whether teachers, coaches, parents, or bosses) didn't get the memo. Because of the amount of things on your plate, it can be challenging to figure out how and when it's all going to come together. If you're adding something new to the mix—a new project, a new goal, a new To Do—you have to figure out how and when you're going to squeeze it all in.

Defense Strategy: It's important to look at how you spend your time. Are you engaging in time sucks that aren't moving you closer to what you want to do? I'm not suggesting you eliminate all fun or chill time from your life. On the contrary, I think those things are incredibly important, perhaps never more so than when you're working toward a big To Do. But it's the other things—the time scrolling through pics on Instagram, vegging in front of the TV for hours, or spending more time complaining than actually doing—that can get in the way of your hoped-for, productive outcome.

The idea that you don't have enough time is an obstacle to getting started because you are essentially saying, "It can't be done." So the real question then becomes: Is that true? Is it true that you don't have enough time, or is it that you feel so overwhelmed that *There's not enough time* becomes your default setting? If it's *not* true, and in reality you *do* have enough time but you're caught up in a stress frenzy, just remind yourself, often, that you do have time to get it all done. And when you find yourself engaging in your time suck activities, gently redirect yourself back to the task at hand.

If there really *isn't* enough time, then that's a whole other story. Then you have to get real about your schedule—understand exactly how much time you have for everything you need to do and make some choices to support your would-be accomplishments. Here's how:

1. Start by making a list of *everything* on your To Do list, whether it be your school requirements, your job, your chores, your sports or extracurriculars, your social time, your family obligations, your volunteer gigs . . . *whatever.*

2. If you're working on a big To Do that has to take priority, think about what activities you can scale back on in the short term, such as skipping your afterschool clubs when it's time to focus solely on your midterms. If you're just looking to reboot your schedule, go through your list and get rid of anything that feels like it doesn't belong, either because you've outgrown it, you've lost interest, or it just isn't that important to you anymore. This is like cleaning out your closet and purging all those clothes you haven't worn for the past two years. Be honest but brutal. And enjoy. Because eliminating things from your schedule feels really liberating!

3. Take a look at your week. You can make a chart in your journal that looks like the following one, or you can flip to it in your Doable workbook (visit www.debbiereber.com). Write in the obligations you have on different days, along with the approximate chunks of time they take up. For example:

Day of the Week	Obligations/To Dos	Hours/Time
Monday	Volleyball practice	3:30–5:00 PM
Tuesday	Sign Language Club	3:30–4:30 PM
Wednesday	Volleyball practice Piano lessons	3:30–5:00 PM 6:00–7:00 PM
Thursday		
Friday	Volleyball practice Movie and out with friends	3:30–5:00 PM 7:00 PM–?
Saturday	Volunteering Babysitting	9:00 AM–NOON 7:00–11:00 PM
Sunday		

What do you notice about your schedule? Which days are more packed than others? On which days do you have wiggle room to devote time and energy to new To Dos? Where can you find pockets of time to make progress on the things you want to accomplish?

JOURNAL: DIY COACHING—SCHEDULE REBOOT

1. Is it really true that I don't have enough time when I'm trying to accomplish something new? Can I come up with any examples of how I might actually have the time but am using it in other, less productive ways?

2. If it *is* true, what changes can I consider making to clear room in my life for working toward my new goals? What obligations can I cut out or scale back to give me room to prioritize my big To Do?

OBSTACLE: LACK OF INFORMATION

My hunch is that when you know exactly how to do something, you can do it without much stress or uncertainty. (Yes, you may get bored or distracted or lose interest, but you won't get stuck because of a knowledge gap.) But when the thing you're trying to accomplish means you have to explore new, uncharted territory, what you don't know can become your biggest roadblock. The bigger, the hairier, the more aspirational, and the more audacious the goal, the more this obstacle comes into play.

College student Anna Gallagher has an ideal strategy for filling in information gaps. "I like to talk to people who have accomplished the goal that I'm reaching for . . . people who have gone through the process that I'm going through. Talking to them about what obstacles they have encountered helps me be prepared and maybe avoid some difficulties," she explains.

Defense Strategy: When lack of information becomes a barrier to moving forward, there are two ways to handle it:

1. Stay stuck in overwhelm because the unknowns you're facing feel uncomfortable, scary, and too hard to overcome.

   Or . . .

2. Figure out what you need to know in order to do what you want to do, and make a plan to learn it.

Which one would you choose? (I'll give you a hint: only one option leads to the promised land.)

JOURNAL: DIY COACHING— CLOSING THE KNOWLEDGE GAP

1. What is my style for learning about new things? (For example, *research online, read books, ask a mentor,* or *figure it out on my own.*)

2. What is the worst thing that can happen if I move ahead and get stuck because I don't know what comes next? (Answer *honestly* here. Would it be the end of the world or just a minor setback?) Is it worth the risk? Can I figure it out as I go along?

3. What resources can I tap into to fill my knowledge gap? What's my plan for moving forward?

OBSTACLE: LACK OF CONFIDENCE

Confidence is that quality or state of being in which you feel truly capable of doing anything you want to do. If you have lots of it, you're likely to push ahead no matter the risks or fears, because you feel certain you have what it takes to get it done. If you lack it, you might second-guess yourself to the point that you never get past square one.

It's hard to believe twenty-year-old Emily-Anne Rigal, founder of the national nonprofit We Stop Hate, could have ever suffered from a lack of confidence, but she did. When she was in elementary school, Emily-Anne was bullied to the point that she switched schools. She found more acceptance in middle school and high school, but she felt driven to do what she could, through YouTube videos and social media, to help teens feel better about themselves. Each video features messages from other teens that remind viewers that they are perfect and worthy just the way they are. In the four years since she launched her idea, Emily-Anne has, among other things, won a World Youth Summit Award, been a

Nickelodeon HALO Award Honoree, personally impacted and connected with international celebs like Lady Gaga, and been named one of the 150 Most Fearless Women in the World by *Newsweek* magazine. Meanwhile, We Stop Hate's YouTube channel has just tipped the 1 million views mark.

Yet while Emily-Anne was fueled by her passion to build We Stop Hate—she says she worked at creating and growing the nonprofit every free moment of her last years of high school—she had obstacles of her own to conquer. Namely, lack of confidence. As she was trying to build her venture, she had to continuously reach out to people and be persistent in garnering enthusiasm for We Stop Hate, which meant tons of phone calls and emails to people who might have had other things on their minds than her project.

"In the beginning, I found it hard because I didn't want to bother people. I didn't want to be that person who emails them a hundred times, because I thought that was obnoxious. So being okay with emailing someone multiple times and following up and not being afraid of bothering them was really hard for me. It's still a challenge, but now it's better," she says.

Emily-Anne found inspiration through an article about Tyra Banks she read in *Seventeen* magazine, where Tyra says (paraphrasing here) if you can't get in the front door, then go through the window. If the window's locked, go through the chimney. The point is . . . just get in there. "That's something I think about when I'm feeling stuck," Emily-Anne says.

Emily-Anne also turns to one of her many mentors for emotional support when she needs a boost of confidence. "Having someone to go to when I'm stuck really helps," she says. When she's struggling, her mentor Jeanne is quick to point out things Emily-Anne has overcome and helps her see the big picture. "We both started projects that we were trying to get off the ground, so I felt like we were in the same boat," Emily-Anne says, adding that their conversations help her feel less alone, more "normal," and more confident.

Defense Strategy: If low confidence is something you struggle with, practice taking small, safe risks—doings things that are slightly outside your comfort zone but don't have a true downside if things don't go your way. For example, you could try a new food, make a new friend, go to the movies alone, sign up for a 5K race, register for a class about a subject you know nothing about . . . you get the point. Think of these small risks as learning to crawl before you walk and run. With each healthy risk you invest in, you make a deposit in your confidence account.

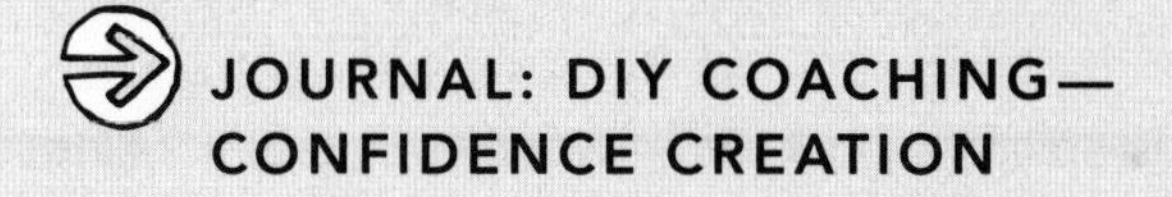

JOURNAL: DIY COACHING—CONFIDENCE CREATION

1. Why do I lack confidence?
2. What are at least five things I'm ridiculously good at?
3. What's the worst thing that could happen if things don't go the way I hope?
4. What risks have I taken in the past that turned out okay?

Set Up for Success

In their book *Switch: How to Change Things When Change is Hard*, authors Chip and Dan Heath write about what it takes to make a change—whether it's in a company, in our own lives, or in the world. In their three-step approach to change, the Heath brothers talk about "shaping the path," which they describe as tweaking our environments to set ourselves up for success. We can apply this same approach to achieve the things we set out to do. When we're working toward something we know is bound to trigger our usual procrastination tendencies or other obstacles, we can shape our paths by adapting our environments, both externally and internally, to propel us toward success.

So, where do you stand? Are your defenses built up? Do you have some positive new truths to focus on? Do you have a handful of strategies to use in proactively facing your regular roadblocks? Good. Because chances are, the things that keep you stuck today—whether crappy thinking, overwhelm, or distractions—are the same things that have always gotten in your way. And they'll continue to do so until you take the time to understand them and decide to change them. Because the truth is, they're nothing more than habits, just like chewing your fingernails, cracking your knuckles, or perpetually running late. You can change your habits. Not only that, but new habits—*better* habits—can be formed. It just takes a little practice.

STEP 3 SUMMARY

It's clear that getting your mind on board for the task at hand is a huge part of making progress toward any goal. But to truly set yourself up for success, you have to couple your new thinking with being proactive about potential obstacles. But don't worry—there are defense strategies to plan ahead for what you know is going to come up.

Step 1: Define Your To Do 

Step 2: Detail the Little Tasks 

Step 3: Defend against Obstacles
Get to know the kinds of obstacles that typically thwart your awesome plans anytime you're trying to get something done—overwhelm, distraction, crappy thinking, stress about time, lack of information, lack of confidence, and so on. Then come up with a plan for beating them before they even start. Some keys to mastering this step are:

- **Understand your personal procrastination triggers.** What are the usual reasons you put things off? For example, *I don't have enough information, I don't have enough time, I don't know how to break it down, I am afraid of screwing up, I don't have a strategy for getting it done, or I always lose momentum.*

- **Use DIY Coaching to overcome procrastination and other obstacles.** Your self-coaching looks different depending on the obstacle, but it always includes an exploration of your:

- **Reasons:** Ask yourself why you do what you do (or in some cases, don't do what you want to do).
- **Emotions:** Explore the not-so-great emotions that accompany those reasons.
- **Thoughts:** Uncover the thoughts that cause those emotions.
- **Reality:** Challenge those thoughts by disputing them.
- **New Truth:** Come up with your new truth.

Remember that you can choose to think about things in a way that is optimistic and propels you forward.

- **Defend against tangible obstacles.** These might involve knowledge gaps, scheduling challenges, or environmental distractions. Ask yourself, "How can I prevent myself from stumbling over tangible roadblocks?"

5

STEP 4: DEVELOP SUPPORT SYSTEMS

Have you ever gone on a road trip? If you have, most likely you knew where you were going (your destination) and exactly how you were going to get there (your route and your transportation). But it takes more than a plan, a set of wheels, and the open road in front of you for a road trip to be successful. There is a GPS or map, the occasional pit stop for gas and snacks and bathrooms along the way, a cell phone charger, an iPod playlist, a spare tire in the trunk, and maybe even a AAA card handy in case you run into any problems.

In the past three chapters, you've learned the importance of getting clear on your concrete goal, you've developed a solid plan you can follow to achieve it, and you've considered the possible roadblocks to your success and strategized ways to get past them. But even if you're Little Miss Independent, finding different ways to support yourself is a key component to a successful outcome. This support can come in various forms, but its purpose is always the same: to get all the energy moving in the right direction so you're more likely to reach your goal.

This is the sentiment behind step 4 of the Doable process—Develop Support Systems—and in this chapter, we'll take a look at what exactly that means as well as how you can tap into all the support already available to you.

A New Definition of Support

When people think of support, their minds tend to go right to financial support (such as borrowing money from our folks) or people pitching in to help someone (feel free to break into an a cappella version of "Lean on Me"). But there are many more ways you can connect with available support to bolster your chances of completing your To Do—you just have to think creatively and ask yourself this question: what support already exists that can help me achieve my goal?

When Sarah Cronk first got The Sparkle Effect up and running, she had a partner in crime, a copresident named Sarah Herr. The girls had different strengths that helped them balance one another out.

"[Sarah Herr] was an incredibly talented cheerleader and was the perfect instructor, so whenever we were working with teens, she knew exactly how to run the most effective training possible," Sarah Cronk says. "She was great at working with kids with disabilities—you know, on the spot like that—but my stronger areas were more behind the scenes. So that really worked out for us in the beginning, and we learned how to play off of each other's strengths."

Sarah Herr left the organization after she graduated, but Sarah Cronk has continued to get the support she needs from those around her. "We wouldn't have gotten anywhere close to where we are now without our amazing corporate sponsors who do things like help us with free advertising and promotional pushes, and our board of directors who bring valuable insight and direction to the organization, especially with regards to nonprofit management, ability activism, and legal responsibilities. And we now have an entire team of trainers, and we've been sending people to different locations all summer long. So we've grown into this incredible team that also has different strengths in different areas."

For go-getters on a mission like Sarah, other people—aka human resources—are probably the greatest source of support. And the good news is, most people truly *like* helping other people. In fact, science shows that being someone who helps others is one of the biggest predictors of happiness. In the book *Why Good Things Happen to Good People: The Exciting New Research that Proves the Link Between Doing Good and Living a Longer, Healthier, Happier Life*, authors Stephen Post and Jill Neimark quote a study which found that "teens who are giving, hopeful, and socially effective are also happier and more active, involved, excited, and challenged than their less engaged counterparts." The evidence just gets stronger as people get older. The bottom line is that helping others is good for people.

Whether your To Do involves helping others or not, don't hesitate to accept support. By letting others help you, you're helping them be happier! Even the smallest To Dos can be supported with a little outside personal help. But to tap into this form of good-for-the-soul support and make it work for you, you have to know *who to ask* and *what to ask for.*

Collaboration

The Who

Let's start with the Who. Chances are, potential help is everywhere. Just look around and you'll likely find some of these types of people, who would love not only to see you succeed but also to be a part of helping you get there:

Mentors: Mentors are people who volunteer their time and energy to advise, guide, and steer others in the right direction when it comes to school, work, relationships, future dreams . . . life. Whether you connect with a formal mentor through an organization like the Girl Scouts or Step Up or the Fulfillment Fund, or you've simply identified someone you admire who plays that role in your life, your mentors have an emotional stake in whether or not you succeed. They're mentors because they *want* to be. They want to have an impact; they are often driven to give back as a way of honoring their own personal mentors, and, chances are, they'll be eager to step up to the plate and support you however they can.

"I think it's really important to find adults outside of your family who are supportive," says college student Anna Gallagher, "so I go out to tea or for a walk with one of my neighbors. She's in her late forties and she used to be a high school counselor, so she's quite interested in my age group. She was someone I would talk to throughout the college admissions process. She doesn't have the same attachment as a parent, so it's sometimes more honest. An outside voice is good to hear, and I've found her to be a great support system for me."

Teachers: Hopefully you have at least one of those teachers who is the stuff movie characters are modeled after—you know, the ones who would walk through fire for their students and whose passion for helping students is abundantly clear by the way they teach their classes and connect with their kids. If you have one of those, even if it's a former teacher from another year, you're good to go.

For Sahar Osmani—college student, Air Force ROTC member, and president of SDSU's chapter of the Coaching Corps—that teacher is her freshman English teacher. "Even when he became assistant principal, he used to pull me out of class just to check in on me, and I would sit and talk to him. I would have lunch with him every once in a while. After I graduated, he was the one person that I still kept in touch with via email. Or when I go back home, I have lunch with him and just catch up. He's constantly asking me about, you know, how my grades are doing, how everything's going down here in San Diego. And it's really cool. Really positive," she says.

Friends: True friends want to see you succeed, and if you need extra hands to tackle your To Do, enlisting the help of your friends is a no-brainer. Depending on what you're doing, more hands can mean quicker results, or at the very least, a better chance of succeeding.

Recent college graduate Cammy Nelson has created a little support posse of five close friends whom she reaches out to for feedback and guidance on all her schemes and dreams. "When I come up with an idea, I send it to them and get their feedback. And if they say, 'Well, you know, it sounds cool, but it needs a little more work,' I'll work on it." For example, while coming up with fundraising ideas for her student organization in college, Cammy shared an idea with her friends, an idea she believed was, in her words, *genius*. But her friends stared back blankly, one of them ever-so-kindly saying, "Um, Cam, I don't really see the hook in that." And so that idea was scratched. Cammy goes on, "They're not afraid to tell me the truth and just say, 'I'm totally confused about what you're talking about right now.' They're people who have seen me through the highs and lows of almost everything, so they know how to deal with me." Wow, who wouldn't love a posse like that?

Parents or Caregivers: The people charged with raising you are an organic part of your support system, whether they explicitly help you on your big To Dos or work behind the scenes to meet your basic needs of food, clothing, and shelter while you're busy kicking ass in your own life. And don't underestimate their desire to help you move toward your goal in any way they can!

Coaches: Whether you're on a sports or academic team or you have your own life coach, coaches are passionate about getting the best performance out of the students they work with. And depending on the goal you're working toward, they may be directly involved in helping you reach it. Coaches, like mentors, do what they do because they love to play a role in inspiring, motivating, and supporting others. Why not take advantage of that?

Librarians: If you're looking for help researching pretty much anything, librarians are an often-overlooked source. Librarians are masters of information—they generally know exactly where to look to find what you need to know. And if they don't, they'll work tirelessly until they can get you answers. (It's what they love to do . . . who knew?)

Tutors: If you're working toward a specific academic goal—getting better grades, making honor roll, scoring high on the SATs—there are people out there whose very business is helping you reach your goals. You can find tutors for just about any subject, so by enlisting their help, you give yourself the gift of powerful, specific support. And who wouldn't want that?

Hopefully by now you have some ideas about who you could reach out to as you work toward your own goals. If you want to take it a step further, you can create a shortlist of your to-turn-to people—that way, anytime you're feeling like you're on your own trying to reach your goals, you can whip out your list and be reminded of the support team that's just a text message away.

The What

So we've covered the Who. Now let's look at the What—as in, what exactly are you asking people to do for you?

Of course, much of the time, this depends on what you're trying to do. For example, if you're having trouble finding sources for a term paper, you might ask your local librarian for strategies to uncover more research. If you're running for student council president, you might ask your friends to help you campaign, or ask a mentor to give you feedback on your debate strategy. Sometimes it's just extra muscle—able bodies to help you lift or lug or move or do anything that requires physical, tangible help. And sometimes it's just emotional support—someone to be your personal cheerleader and keep you going even when you start to lose faith.

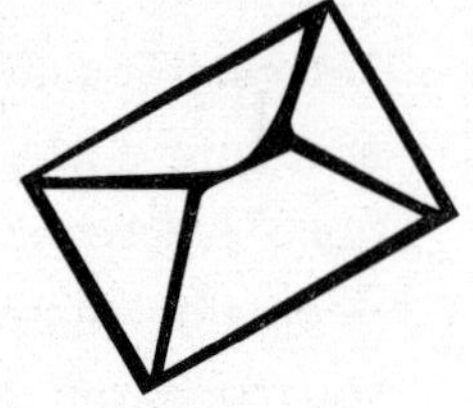

When you ask for support from others, be sure to tell them exactly what you need them to do. For example, if your friend offered to help you put up decorations for your end-of-the-school-year party, give her the supplies and show her samples of how you want it done. Otherwise your visions might clash, and come party time, you'll be wondering why your backyard is full of candles and flowers instead of tiki torches and leis. Without direction, well-meaning helpers may end up creating more work for you or getting you off track, which will only result in frustration all around.

There is another way others can help us accomplish what we set out to do. It isn't as apparent as tangible help, but it's one of the most effective tools you can have in your Doable arsenal: *accountability*. Accountability is essentially making yourself responsible to someone or something. For some people, being accountable to themselves is all it takes—they set goals and work toward them without any problems because they don't want to let themselves down. But for the rest of us? Being accountable to another person can be a tremendous influence in helping us reach what we're after. It's based on the idea of social expectations: when another person or a group of people expects us to do something, most of the time we feel compelled to meet that expectation. While I'm not one to give too much weight to what other people think about what I do, I've found accountability to be an incredibly powerful tool for getting stuff done.

Building accountability into your To Dos doesn't have to be a big deal. It might be as simple as asking someone to check in on your progress with the occasional friendly nudge. For example, you could say to a mentor or teacher or friend, "Hey, I need to finish my resume by May 1 so I can apply for a decent summer job. Can you ask me about it by April 25 to see how I'm doing?" Boom—instant accountability. Or at the very least, a reminder system that will allow you to still hit your deadline, even if you haven't taken action by the time your friend checks in.

There are also many organizations that have their own built-in accountability component, like Junior Achievement, the Girl Scouts, and Step Up. By showing up for regular meetings where you'll be asked to report your progress, you're providing yourself with a framework for accountability.

Marni Bates uses accountability a lot in her day-to-day life, especially as a way to tackle her procrastination tendencies. She is part of a small community of writers who keep everybody honest as they work on their respective books. She explains, "One of us will say, 'Hey, we're each going to write nine thousand words by Wednesday, and if you don't make it you're not allowed to read romance novels,' or 'you're not allowed to watch the Disney Channel.' We try and come up with punishments that will make us want to keep going with our stuff."

My favorite form of accountability is a go-big-or-go-home approach: publicly declare on social media exactly what you plan to do and ask your online community to help you stick to it. For example, say you've signed up for your first 5K, but you regularly struggle getting your training runs in. You know that if you don't put in the time to train, race day isn't going to feel so hot. You could post an update on Facebook like, "Don't feel like heading out for my run today . . . rain, cold, bleh. Need a little push . . . can you help me out?" In no time, your

TEAM

Facebook friends will be urging you on and you'll be further fueled to lace up and get out there. There's nothing better than reporting in after your run with a "Thanks all . . . killed it!"

As you map out your plan of attack for plugging ahead toward your goal, think about who in your network of people—from family and friends to acquaintances and authority figures in your life—might be just the perfect person to step up to the plate, have your back, and maybe even give you a metaphorical kick in the pants if and when you need it.

YOUR SUPPORT PLAN: PART 1

For each goal you're working toward, support yourself by getting clear on your Who and What when it comes to how others can play roles in your pursuit. Grab your journal or flip open your Doable workbook and fill in the following.

1. **Your Goal:** Write down the name of the goal you are working toward.

2. **Your Who:** Write down the names of your go-to people . . . those people who will always go out of their way to help you anytime you need support. Of your go-to people, whom do you want to reach out to for help with this goal? Is there anyone else outside your circle who is perfectly positioned to support you and might be willing to help?

3. **Your What:** What kind of support would best help you achieve your goal? Describe your ideal support for each of the following categories:

- Emotional (confidence boosts, pep talks)
- Physical (hands-on, tangible support)
- Accountability (check-ins, deadline tracking)

4. **Put It All Together:** Go through your list of people you want to reach out to and write down the specific kind of help you plan to ask each person for. For example:

- *Denelle James: Design the logo and poster for my photography stand at the art show*
- *Kevin Ellis: Help me hand out flyers after school*
- *Ms. Boyle: Advise me on the color corrections of my photo proofs*

Organizations and Clubs

No matter what you're looking to do, I'd bet good money that you could find a related organization, website, or community that just might be an ideal resource. Whether you're working on starting your own business, designing a website, finding the perfect volunteer gig, or learning how to *parler français*, find out what kinds of resources already exist that can put you on the fast track to your final destination. Here are just a few ideas to get you thinking about the types of sources of information and motivation you can tap into.

SPECIALTY ORGANIZATIONS AND NONPROFITS

Like-minded people who share a passion or interest often join forces and create formal communities. Sometimes these are small, local grassroots efforts, and sometimes they're mega-global movements.

There are, as I mentioned earlier, the biggies—large national or international organizations designed to support young women in pursuing their dreams. Girl Scouts, Girls Inc., Step Up, Girls for a Change, Girl Talk, and others like them have tools and programs specifically designed around the types of goals you might be pursuing. As a bonus, they often have built-in accountability in the form of mentorship, and some have reward systems to spark your motivation (earn a Girl Scouts badge lately?). And then there are smaller local or regional organizations or nonprofits that might be a perfect match for what you're trying to do.

For example, say Ariel lives in Los Angeles and dreams of being a professional screenwriter someday. She already has tons of ideas for screenplays she'd like to write, and she's read (and practically memorized) the bible of the screenwriting industry, the book *Story* by Robert McKee. But Ariel needs help applying what she's read to her actual script writing. Plus, through her self-discovery work in step 3, Ariel has recognized that while she's really good at *starting* screenplays, one of her typical obstacles is not finishing any of her projects.

After a little poking around online, Ariel discovered WriteGirl, an LA-based nonprofit that partners women writers with teen girls for creative writing and mentorship. A quick look at WriteGirl's website shows that the organization offers a workshop on character and dialogue, and many of the mentors are screenwriters, so there is a good chance Ariel could be paired with a working Hollywood screenwriter for one-on-one mentoring. Now Ariel has found the ideal support partner, and before she knows it, she'll be typing the words *The End* for the first time ever!

But organizational support extends beyond those groups designed specifically around mentoring and supporting girls. Organizations and movements exist around pretty much *any* interest, and tapping into the resources they already have in place can buoy you toward success.

Say McCauley is passionate about bringing clean water to villages in sub-Saharan Africa. Making an impact on her own would be incredibly difficult, unless her mom is an ambassador and she has direct access to aid organizations who need her help. But what if she's recently learned about Charity: Water, a global nonprofit whose sole purpose is bringing safe drinking water to every person on the planet? Now McCauley can focus her efforts on creating a campaign or raising funds to sponsor a well in the developing country of her choice. McCauley's To Do list just got more streamlined and concrete. She only has to do her part and Charity: Water, will do the rest, using 100 percent of the money McCauley raises to fund water projects.

CLUBS

Informal clubs that get together over shared interests are another way to connect with people and gain support as you work toward your goals. You can find Meetups in every city and town, based on any area of interest you can imagine. These groups bring together people for anything from learning obscure forms of exercise to reading similar books, from singing show tunes or participating in flash mobs to cleaning up the beach. (And if you can't find a Meetup that suits your needs, you can always form your own!)

Depending on the To Do you're tackling, consider whether or not surrounding yourself with people working toward the same goal might give you the extra oomph you need to reach a successful conclusion. Then set about to finding your people. Besides Meetups, you can see if there are clubs—at your school, in your community, or online—built around your thing. Want to participate in a poetry jam? Join a poetry club. Want to enter the Google Science Fair? Hook up with the Science Club for Girls. You get the point.

VIRTUAL HANGOUTS

Some people say being continuously plugged in—to our smartphones, our tablets, our computers, our iPods—has made us disconnected as a society. Me? I think our society and communities just look different today than they did in generations past. Today, with one click of a button, we can connect in a very real way with people from around the world, united by a cause, an ideal, or a passion. As of the writing of this book, there are 620 million groups on Facebook. There are 10 million LISTSERVs on Yahoo! Groups. That's *a lot* of groups. And that's just two social networking tools. Add Twitter, Pinterest, and the millions of online-only environments rich in content, information, and connection, and anyone looking for support in making a goal more doable doesn't have to go far to find it.

TECHNOLOGY AND SYSTEMS

Have you ever heard of the saying, "You don't need to reinvent the wheel"? That adage is the friend of would-be Doers because it reminds us to take advantage of existing technology that can specifically, and efficiently, move us closer to our goals. For example, if your goal is to start a blog, why not start a Tumblr or grab a free plug-and-post template from WordPress? All you have to do is add your content and you're off. There's no need to write your own HTML code for a brand-new website. Or if you want to add a half-mile distance to your run each week, MapMyRun does all the work of measuring out a route for you. Maybe you want to eliminate Monsanto foods from your diet. There's an app for that too—rather than research all the manufacturers of the food you eat, scan the barcodes on food labels with the Buycott app, which lets you know if the food is in the clear.

While it would take me a very long time to name all the different technological resources available that might support you in doing what you want to do (and I would definitely miss my deadline to my publisher if I tried to do so), my hope is that the following list will help get you started thinking creatively about how you can use existing technology, systems, and applications to help you reach your goals. Here's just a taste:

- **Reminder and Tracking Apps:** There are hundreds of thousands of smartphone apps available, many for free and others for just a buck or two, and lots are designed to simplify your life in some way, shape, or form. Thousands of apps help you track your progress as you work toward goals, while others send you reminders about just about anything. For example, apps like 30/30 help you set a time limit for any activity so you can balance your chill time with your getting-down-to-business time. For the health-conscious Doer, MyNetDiary tracks your meals and workouts, and even makes sure you drink enough water each day. There's even an app that sends you reminders for when it's time to water your plants (perfect for the student with no green thumb who volunteered to babysit the class plant over summer break). Whatever you're looking to do, chances are, there's an app for that.

- **Auto This and That:** If your goal has multiple tasks that need to be repeated frequently, see if you can eliminate the amount of time you spend on them by using automated systems. For example, could setting up auto replies through your email account get you closer to your goal of cleaning out your email inbox by the end of winter break? Could a shopping cart widget on your website automatically handle orders and payments from the people who purchase your cool, homemade products?

- **Software and Websites:** Software for your computer or tablet, along with specialty, service-based websites, has made it much simpler to do what used to take days or weeks to accomplish. Graphic design programs like Photoshop and Fireworks are ideal if you're designing posters, T-shirts, websites, logos, and more. Book organization software like Scrivener takes the chaos out of novel writing. Rosetta Stone DVD language programs have made mastering another language a totally doable solo venture. Translations and conversions can be done in a nanosecond for free through Google or online conversion calculators. As you lay out all the little steps you need to take to accomplish your goal, ask yourself: are there existing sites, platforms, or programs that would speed up or simplify my process?

- **Free and Cheap Technology:** Even if you don't have your own computer, tablet, or smartphone, you can still access tech goodness by tapping into local services and organizations that provide free or low-cost hardware and software. For example, you can drop in at a local library to get online—all you need is a library card and you're good to go. If you're looking for specialized tech tools such as high-cost graphic design or animation programs, look for local organizations or community centers that offer training as well as access to expensive programs for free or for a low annual membership fee.

PRODUCTS AND SUPPLIES

Okay, I'll fess up. I *love* me some office supplies. Set me loose in a Staples or OfficeMax and in no time my basket will be overflowing with funky-designed folders, a plethora of notebooks, multicolored pens, and neon Post-its. I'm not sure why I love office supplies so much, but I know part of it is that they make my life easier. Not only do my file folders, notebooks, and related office supplies help me get organized and create structure around my To Dos, but because I buy supplies with designs I love, the very act of using them becomes more enjoyable.

Of course, the specific products and supplies you might need for your To Dos will vary greatly depending on what it is you're taking on. But here are just a few ideas for the kinds of things many goal getters use to help make their tasks more achievable:

- **Books:** Are there any books out there that could help you plan, figure out, or execute your To Do? Check out your local bookstore, the school or public library, or Amazon.

- **Notebooks and Journals:** Would dedicating a notebook to your goal help you be more organized in taking the steps you need to take?

- **Pens and Writing Implements:** What kinds of writing instruments would support you in your project? Highlighters? Different colored pens or markers? Mechanical pencils?

- **Whiteboard:** Would keeping track of your schedule or progress on a giant whiteboard mounted to your wall keep you motivated and on task?

- **Post-Its:** Could you benefit from scribbling reminders, brain dumps, and daily To Dos on sticky notes and posting them on your bulletin board, desk, or bedroom wall?

Getting the Support You Need

So let's take a step back. We've covered the Who (who to ask) and the What (what to ask for). But there's still the How, as in, how should I ask for help? This is where many people get hung up, as the actual asking-for-help part can be difficult, especially for people who are super independent or like to do it all themselves.

Why is asking others for help so challenging to so many? There is a misguided notion floating around out there that asking for help is a sign of weakness . . . that it makes us vulnerable by letting others see that we can't do everything on our own. Well, yes. It may make us vulnerable, but who says that's a bad thing? Author and researcher Brené Brown has spent years discovering the key to living a "wholehearted life," which she describes as a life in which one has a strong sense of love and belonging. Much to her surprise, she found that vulnerability is actually at the core of such a life. She says wholehearted living is "going to bed at night thinking, *Yes, I am imperfect and vulnerable and sometimes afraid, but that doesn't change the truth that I am also brave and worthy of love and belonging.*" So by asking for help, we're actually improving the quality of our lives.

The truth is, asking for help doesn't make us weaker . . . it makes us *stronger*. We learn from our supporters, and that makes us more capable, more empowered, and more likely to reach our goals. There's no way we can all be good at everything—even the most powerful people in the world have support teams to back them up and pick up the slack where and when they need it. So let's just put the ridiculous idea that asking for help is a sign of weakness to rest once and for all, shall we?

When you *do* ask for help, whether you're looking for moral support, advice and guidance, or hands-on manual labor, here are some guidelines for how to do so in a way that will yield the most positive results but also allow you to feel good about it, no matter how the person answers:

- **Be authentic:** When you're asking for help, let people know what's really going on with you—why reaching your To Do is so important to you. Authenticity connects with people on an emotional level, and the emotional part of the brain is where all the decision-making processes are centered. So allow yourself to be vulnerable and authentic when you're reaching out for help, and people who identify with what you're trying to do will feel compelled to support you. For example, if you're organizing a neighborhood art walk, let people know why you're doing it—to get exposure as a painter and connect with other artists—and tell them how you feel about the goal—nervous about pulling it off, excited to follow your passion, or scared no one will show up. Let people in and they'll be more likely to get behind you.

- **Be transparent:** Let people know exactly what you're asking of them and why you chose them. For example, if you're targeting someone because of her connections, that's okay . . . just be honest and up front about it. For example, for the neighborhood art walk, you might reach out to your mom's colleague who is totally connected to the local art scene and ask her if you can drop her name when you're talking to galleries about participation. When you're transparent with your requests, people can respond knowing what they're getting into, and you'll know that if they say yes, it's because they really want to.

- **Be bold:** The best way to ask for something is to *just ask*. It's not necessary to sugar coat, prep, include disclaimers, or come up with fancy ways to convey what would be most helpful. You know what you need—like the Nike ad says, just do it. Or in this case, just ask. Bold requests start with words like: "I need your help," or "Can you do _____ for me?" For example, "Can you call five galleries and personally invite them to attend my art walk?"

- **Be creative:** Sometimes the person you want to ask is a professional—for example, a graphic designer or a coach—who would typically be paid for this . . . which you may not have the money to do. If that's the case, think creatively about how else you might be able to secure this person's assistance. For example, you could offer to trade one of your original paintings in exchange for someone's help setting up an art walk website.

- **Be okay if they say no:** Placing expectations on others sets ourselves up for disappointment. Even if we think someone owes us or should help us when we ask, the great thing about being an individual is that we all get to decide what we want to do and how we want to feel about it. So part of that means being okay if others say no. When people decline to help you, try not to make it about you. (Watch for thoughts that sound like, *She must not like me*, or *If he were my real friend, he would do anything for me*, and so on.) People are dealing with their own stuff, and the decisions they make always reflect what's going on in their own minds and worlds. It's not about you.

- **Be grateful and respectful when people say yes:** As you ask for help, people will undoubtedly step up to the plate to support you. Sometimes this help is exactly what you asked for, and other times it might not be what you originally had in mind but the helper's intention is still to see you succeed. However people support you, be respectful of their time and make sure they know how much you appreciate their help. Assume they're helping you because they care about you and want to see you thrive, and thank them with a handwritten note, a thoughtful email, or even a heartfelt personal thank-you.

YOUR SUPPORT PLAN: PART 2

Earlier in this chapter, you determined Who to approach for support and What exactly to ask for. Now it's time to come up with a plan for How to ask for that support in a way that not only moves you toward your goal but also feels positive and stress-free. Take a few minutes to answer the following questions and come up with a plan that works for you.

1. **Authenticity:** Why is achieving this goal so important for you on a deep, cellular level? How can you share your personal motivation in a way that will connect with those you are turning to for help?

2. **Transparency:** What are your reasons for reaching out to the people on your list? What makes them your ideal supporters as you work toward this goal? How will you communicate this to the people you reach out to?

3. **Boldness:** What is the exact language you will use in making your request? What is your plan for asking for what you need without any disclaimers, excuses, or wordy buildups?

4. **Creativity:** If you need professional support, what creative ways can you come up with to secure this person's help? Is there an opportunity for a trade or barter?

5. **Ready for Anything:** How will you respond if people say no? How will you respond if people say yes?

In her book *The Gifts of Imperfection*, Dr. Brené Brown quotes her friend, author Katherine Center: "You have to be brave with your life so that others can be brave with theirs." So be brave. Ask for help. It's not just good sense . . . it's good all around. Good for those you ask, good for your goal, and good for you.

STEP 4 SUMMARY

In today's world of complete and utter interconnectedness, one thing is for certain: *we are not alone*. This is good news for anyone tackling a To Do, and embracing this notion will take you far. You just have to be willing to ask for, and be open to, the different forms support might take. When you are, who knows just how easy your Doable task might become?

Step 1: Define Your To Do ✓

Step 2: Detail the Little Tasks ✓

Step 3: Defend against Obstacles ✓

Step 4: Develop Support Systems
By soliciting support in various forms—hands-on, emotional, technological, organizational—we are effectively harnessing the resources available to get all the energy around us moving in the same direction. And we want that

direction to be one that greatly increases the chances that we will reach our goals. Here are a few tips for connecting with that energy and taking advantage of other forms of support:

- **Tap into the people around you who can play a role in helping you succeed.** These include mentors, teachers, friends, coaches, parents, librarians, and tutors. Make a short-list of your go-to people so you are ready to reach out when the time comes.

- **Be specific about the kind of support you need.** Make sure well-intentioned helpers know exactly what you need them to do, or you might end up running behind schedule or find yourself further from reaching your goal.

- **Find ways to build accountability into your support process.** You could be accountable either to yourself or to someone or something else. Ask a friend to check in with you, report to an organization or club, or go public and rely on your social media community for accountability.

- **Explore and connect with organizations and clubs whose missions and purposes are in alignment with what you're trying to do.** Look for specialty organizations and nonprofits, virtual and otherwise, perfectly positioned to bring you closer to your goal.

- **Take advantage of existing technology and products that can efficiently move you closer to your goal.** From free blogware, reminder apps, and goal-specific software to books and office supplies, opportunities abound.

- **Get comfortable asking for help and know that doing so is a sign of strength, not weakness.** Be authentic (people who identify with what you're trying to do will feel compelled to support you), be transparent (let people know what you're asking and why you chose them), be bold (just ask), be creative (consider trades and barters), be okay if they say no (it's about them, not you), and be grateful and respectful when people say yes (thank them).

6

STEP 5: DETERMINE WHAT SUCCESS LOOKS LIKE

When Ella Viscardi started her fashion blog, *Ella Etcetera*, she knew she wanted to take her interests in art, fashion, and music online so she could share them with people. Over time, she realized that her passion for fashion was emerging as the clear focus, and so she shifted her blog to reflect that. But she didn't necessarily know if or when she'd be successful, nor did she know what success actually meant to her.

"In the beginning, I kind of thought that success was measured by how many followers I had or how many comments I was getting. Today I still don't have thousands of people reading my blog, but I have been recognized by websites like *Teen Vogue* and Refinery 29, and for me personally those are huge successes."

Ella's story spotlights what one of the most important, yet often ignored, parts of going after goals is—determining what success or completion looks like. For some To Dos, recognizing success is a no-brainer, but for many amorphous goals, success can live in a fuzzy gray area or, even more tricky, be dependent on what other people think or feel. In order for a To Do to be truly attainable, you've got to get über clear on how you'll know you've achieved it. I talked about this briefly in Step 1: Defining Your To Do, but this is such an important factor in achieving what you set out to do that it warrants its own chapter.

What *Is* Success?

Think about the concept of success. People talk about wanting to be successful in their lives, but what does being successful actually mean? Does it mean making a lot of money or having a fabulous house or car or wardrobe? Or is it about going to an Ivy League college, getting a prestigious degree, and fearlessly rising through the ranks of a fabulous career path? Maybe to you being successful means having a positive impact on the world or living a simple life with a perfect balance of work and play. Whatever it is, your definition of success is likely different from that of your friends and family—it's not a one-size-fits-all kind of thing. How you perceive success is likely connected to your value system and reflects your personal priorities.

The same idea applies to goals and To Dos. In chapter 2, we looked at the goal of wanting to be a good soccer player. When we applied our technique for making vague goals more concrete, we were easily able to get specific about what we might want to do. We decided that being a good soccer player could mean scoring more consistently; being an expert juggler, dribbler, passer, receiver, and/or shooter; or having enough stamina to last an entire game.

But as we discussed, the only way to know you've *successfully achieved* your goal is to figure out what that definition of success is for you—and only you—in relation to that specific goal. Determining what success looks like shouldn't be an afterthought of goal pursuing, and it isn't just for vague goals, either. It is a practice that should be built into *every single* goal and To Do you work toward.

Let's see how this Doable step works when applied to real goals. Here's a list of ten different To Dos that teen girls told me they were working toward when I was researching for this book:

Goal
I want to be on time for work.
I want to improve my SAT score.
I want to learn Spanish.
I want to earn enough money to buy a used car.
I want to make honor roll.
I want to ask my crush to be my date for prom.
I want to change the world.
I want to be nicer to my sister.
I want to travel to NYC.
I want to become a better photographer.

As you can see, some of these goals are more concrete than others, so before we do anything else, let's apply Doable step 1—Define Your To Do—to these goals so we know exactly what it is these girls want to accomplish. Here's what this step might look like were we to dig deeper into these goals:

Goal	Defining the To Do
I want to be on time for work.	I want to leave 10 minutes earlier for work so I can arrive 5 minutes before my shift begins . . . every time!
I want to improve my SAT score.	I want to boost my SAT scores in all three sections by at least 50 points each.
I want to learn Spanish.	I want to go through the entire Rosetta Stone Spanish Level 1 DVD this summer so I can speak conversational Spanish.
I want to earn enough money to buy a used car.	I want to save up $2,000 to buy a used car.
I want to make honor roll.	I want to get all As this quarter so I make honor roll for the first time!
I want to ask my crush to be my date for prom.	(No change.)
I want to change the world.	I want to regularly volunteer for organizations that are working toward eliminating poverty.
I want to be nicer to my sister.	I want to stop yelling at my sister, be more patient with her, and stop getting in trouble for fighting with her.

I want to travel to NYC.	I want to save enough money to take the train to NYC and see a Broadway show before I graduate from high school.
I want to become a better photographer.	I want to take a photography class at the Art Institute this summer and start taking more photos.

Now we can see exactly what each To Do looks like so we can get started. These Doers are ready to take action! Except . . . we still don't know what achieving those goals actually means. As you can see from the following breakdown, what a successful outcome looks like is super straightforward for some, while for others, not so much.

Goal	Defining the To Do	What Success Looks Like
I want to be on time for work.	I want to leave 10 minutes earlier for work so I can arrive 5 minutes before my shift begins . . . every time!	I will not be written up for being late to work once in the next three months.
I want to improve my SAT score.	I want to boost my SAT scores in all three sections by at least 50 points each.	I will get at least a 660 in math, a 570 in writing, and a 600 in critical reading when I take the SATs again in June.
I want to learn Spanish.	I want to go through the entire Rosetta Stone Spanish Level 1 DVD this summer so I can speak conversational Spanish.	I will go through the entire Level 1 program by August 31 and score above 90 percent on all the exercises.

Goal	Defining the To Do	What Success Looks Like
I want to earn enough money to buy a used car.	I want to save up $2,000 to buy a used car.	I will have my car!
I want to make honor roll.	I want to get all As this quarter so I make honor roll for the first time!	I will make honor roll this quarter.
I want to ask my crush to be my date for prom.	(No change.)	I will have officially asked my crush to go the prom with me by May 1.
I want to change the world.	I want to regularly volunteer for organizations that are working toward eliminating poverty.	By the end of the month, I will be a volunteer with an anti-poverty organization in my community and will be scheduled to volunteer at least two hours a week.
I want to be nicer to my sister.	I want to stop yelling at my sister, be more patient with her, and stop getting in trouble for fighting with her.	I will not argue with my sister more than once a week.
I want to travel to NYC.	I want to save enough money to take the train to NYC and see a Broadway show before I graduate from high school.	I will have traveled to NYC and seen a Broadway show by June 15 after my senior year. (Now the question is, what show should I see?)
I want to become a better photographer.	I want to take a photography class at the Art Institute this summer and start taking more photos.	I will have taken the Advanced Photography class at the AI, and I will be taking at least 20 photographs each week and posting them on my blog.

See what I mean? By taking the time to ruminate on the ideal outcome for each of these examples, success is now a reachable goal—it will be unquestioningly apparent when each girl has achieved success. And when it's time to get down to business, the girls will know exactly where they're headed. So don't skip this step. Do it for every To Do on your plate! I promise it will make the journey toward completion that much smoother, plus you'll know exactly when it's time to break out your party pants and celebrate your accomplishment.

It's All about You

In step 1, we touched on the fact that sometimes you might be working on goals whose success relies on outside factors (meaning, they're not within your control), and we looked at why it's critical that achieving your goal is something that's 100 percent within your power. But if your goals don't start out that way, have no fear. Just like the way we tweaked the vague goals to make them more concrete, we can also rework the outcomes of goals that are focused on others and turn them back to you.

Here are some examples to help you think about how you might apply this filter to your own goals and To Dos:

Goals with Outcomes *beyond* Your Control	**Tweaked Goals with Outcomes *within* Your Control**
Getting a book published	Completing a book and submitting it to publishers for consideration
Getting into your dream college	Meeting the application criteria for your dream college and submitting a strong application
Becoming prom queen	Running for prom queen

THE CONTROL TEST

If you're not sure whether or not the outcome of your goal is within your control, ask yourself if achieving your To Do requires one or more individuals, an organization, or a business to:

- Vote for you
- Endorse you
- Hire you
- Choose you
- Say yes to you

If the answer is yes to any of the above, find a way to shift the power back to you.

To reclaim power over your goal, restate your To Do so it's about the *pursuit* of something (such as *pursuing* a college scholarship) as opposed to the attainment of it (*receiving* the scholarship). You'll go after these kinds of goals with the same drive and motivation as you would any other goal, but this change of focus makes the goal 100 percent within your power . . . 100 percent doable.

This reframe has been an important consideration for teen scientist and researcher Naomi Shah because so many of the things she's working on don't have clear, predictable outcomes—after all, she's conducting scientific experiments.

"There's really no one who has done the research that I'm doing," she explains. "So what I usually do in terms of success is try and define a goal for myself, like, 'Success is if, at the end of this year, I can have some type of result to share with people who can benefit.' It doesn't have to be breakthrough. In research, you can never predict whether your data is going to support your hypothesis. So because of that, you can't really bank on your data proving what you think it'll prove."

If Naomi tied her definition of success to the *outcome* of an experiment, she'd have absolutely no control over whether or not it could be achieved. So she reframes success in a way that works for her.

See It

When I was in high school, track and field was my thing—specifically, the hurdles. By junior year, I was one of the top 100-meter hurdlers in my county (that's *county*, not country!), and I lived, ate, and breathed my race. My particular obsession was trying to convince my less-than-long legs to manage the standard three steps in between each hurdle, which were placed 8.5 meters apart. Four-stepping, which required alternating legs every time I jumped over a hurdle, was what my natural running stride inclined me to do, but I knew I was losing precious time with those extra steps. If I was going to compete with the big girls, I had to find a way to lose that fourth step.

Each year, long before track season started, you could find me doing circuits in the hallway after school. My English teacher, Mr. Bankert, who doubled as a track coach, volunteered his time to help me run drills. Between the drills, the speed workouts, and strength training, I was covering all the bases and doing everything I physically could to improve my chances of reaching my goal. But would it be enough?

Enter *Chariots of Fire*. I watched the 1982 Academy Award-winning movie (based on the inspiring true story of two track and field runners in the 1924 Olympics) over and over and over, and soon I was obsessed with the signature soundtrack by Vangelis. That soundtrack was the background to my dreams . . . literally. Each night I'd play the soundtrack and, as I drifted off to sleep, I'd let the music guide me in a visual meditation in which I totally nailed the three-step. I'd picture my race: stepping into the starting blocks, hearing the sound of the starting gun, lurching forward toward the first hurdle, perfectly clearing the wooden obstacle, and then step-step-step-hurdle over the next one. Down the lane I'd go, powering through, feeling stronger with each stride.

This listen-and-dream pattern became my nightly ritual. I don't think I even realized that I was creating emotional memories and emotional energy that tangibly increased my chances of making my vision a reality. But I did it, and it worked. Though three-stepping between hurdles was something I always had to work hard to do, I did it, especially in the races where it mattered.

Earlier in this chapter, we explored the importance of being specific about what accomplishing our goals and To Dos looks like. *I won't be written up for being late for work once in the next three months*, or *I will have traveled to NYC and seen a Broadway show by June 15 after my senior year.*

But really serious goal getters take their efforts to a whole other level by focusing not just on what accomplishing the goal will *look* like but also what it will actually *feel* like—just like I did with three-stepping those hurdles. When you can tap into your emotional side as you pursue a goal, you're much more likely to reach it.

Not to get all woo woo on you, but there is plenty of evidence out there to show that what we think about becomes what we experience. As Dr. Srinivasan Pillay, author of *Life Unlocked*, explains, "The brain regions involved in 'intention' are very connected to those regions involved in action. As a result, firing up those brain regions involved in intention will start to fire up your action centers." This is part of the foundation for the law of attraction, the quantum mechanics theory that was made popular around the world by the movie and book *The Secret*.

Whether you buy into the ideas behind the law of attraction or not, it's hard to argue with the idea that what we think about becomes our experience, at least on some level. Think about all the Debbie Downers and Negative Nellies you know. Doesn't it seem like they continue to attract more crappy stuff into their lives, while people who focus on the positive just seem to find more good things to celebrate everywhere they turn? The same idea applies to pursuing goals and To Dos. If we choose to think about how awesome it will feel when we've accomplished our goals, we're much more likely to achieve them than if we were to spend all our time worrying about what might go wrong or picturing ourselves failing.

Think about it—if I'd spent all my nights in high school lying in my twin bed, dreaming of my race, and picturing myself hitting my knee on each hurdle or catching my foot and sprawling out on the track on my hands and knees, what do you think would have been the likely outcome of my races? Two words: *track rash*.

Write It

Visualizing yourself reaching your goal can provide that extra energy to propel you toward a successful outcome, but to seal the deal, write out exactly what you want to happen.

WRITE NOW!

1. Grab your journal or Doable workbook and flesh out exactly how you'd like the experience to unfold, but with a twist: *Write it as if it's a done deal.* So, instead of jotting down what you *want* to achieve, imagine you've hopped in a time portal and emerged three, six, or twelve months down the road. Then write from your future self's perspective about what you've already achieved.

2. Add in lots of details about how you feel having achieved it. This will marinate your thoughts in all that good energy.

For example, if I had done this for my goal of wanting to be a three-step hurdler, it might have looked something like this:

It's the end of track season, and I'm so psyched that I ran my 100-meter hurdle race at my meets exactly the way I wanted to! Three-stepping in between each hurdle was so much fun, and I felt strong when I did it. I love that I was able to power through each race, and being able to keep up with Mary Gooch at districts was so, so awesome! I'm so happy that I put in all that extra time training and that I reached my goal—it feels incredible!

Collage It

For visual, creative thinkers, vision boards can be a great way to capture the essence of a goal in an artistic way. If you haven't seen one before, a vision board is simply a visual representation of the goal you are trying to reach. The most common way to make a vision board is to create a collage of photographs, images, and words cut from magazines that together create a vision of your hoped-for result.

"Something a lot of my friends do is create vision boards, but to be honest I was perhaps cynical of them in the past. I thought just pasting words and pictures of things isn't going to make them happen, you know—you have to actually work hard and take action," explains Tammy Tibbetts, who was only twenty-three when she started thinking about her nonprofit. Her organization, She's the First, sponsors girls' education in developing nations, giving them the chance to become the first ones in their families to graduate from secondary school. The idea is that they'll go on to positively impact their villages and the world.

But last year Tammy added the creation of vision boards to her other goal-chasing strategies. "I made this vision board and put it on the wall next to my desk at home, and I have to tell you, it's like magic. Things actually did start to happen, and it wasn't because I just glued them to a piece of paper. It's because I see that board every single day in my bedroom, and it helps remind me of what I want to do. . . . You can't underestimate the power of visual reminders."

Tammy achieved her goal of harnessing social media to create tangible social change. She's witnessed the impact firsthand, guiding her organization to help hundreds of girls in the developing world be the first ones in their families to go to college. And though she received the Diane von Furstenberg People's Voice Award in 2013 and was recognized as one of *Glamour's* 20 Young Women Who Are Already Changing the World, Tammy has many more big goals to chase, including writing a book and traveling around the world to work directly with the girls She's the First supports.

Whether you choose to write out your future vision or, like Tammy and her friends, create a vision board, post whatever you create on your wall, on your desk, on your mirror, or in the front of your journal. Just make sure it's somewhere you can see it often. Then, read through it and soak in the words, or take time every day to let your eyes rest on the images you chose and really *feel* those emotions that come up. Doing this even once a day will help keep you focused, positive, and inspired about not only what you're trying to achieve but also why you're doing it and how you will feel once you've accomplished it. And this, my friends, will propel you forward.

SEE IT!

Make your own vision board! It's easy peasy. All you need are some words, some images, a dream, and a little imagination. Here's how:

1. Decide whether or not you want to make a vision board on poster board or create an electronic one on your computer.

2. If you're using poster board, grab some old magazines (ones you can cut up) and flip through them, clipping images and words that somehow connect with your goal. If you're creating a virtual vision board, search for images online and save them in a vision board file.

3. Make a collage with the images and words on your poster board or virtual vision board, the only rule being that there are no rules.

4. Have fun! Your vision board doesn't have to be a literal representation of the goal you're trying to achieve—it just needs to connect with your goal on an emotional level. The point is to create an image that allows you to feel those positive emotions you'll experience when you've reached your goal so you can spend time marinating in that delicious vision every day.

Write it, draw it, collage it, or just envision it—whichever approach you choose, taking the time to clarify your ideal outcome for your goal will make achieving that outcome much more likely. Do it for each goal, and remember—this is your pursuit, and therefore what a successful outcome looks like has to be defined by you . . . and only you.

STEP 5 SUMMARY

People constantly chase after "success," but so few actually take the time to consider their own personal definitions of success or define exactly what successful completion of a goal means. Instead, we tend to get caught up trying to achieve and complete things based on others' points of view or a fuzzy vision of reaching the other side of a goal. When it comes to pursuing goals, figuring out exactly what successful completion means to you is really the only way to move forward in a Doable way.

Step 1: Define Your To Do 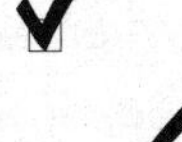

Step 2: Detail the Little Tasks 

Step 3: Defend against Obstacles 

Step 4: Develop Support Systems 

Step 5: Determine What Success Looks Like

Defining what a successful outcome for any goal looks and feels like isn't just a nice thing to do if you have the time. It is a practice that should be built into every single thing you take on. Here are a few things to keep in mind:

- **Make sure your final outcome is something you can measure, track, and check off your list.** For example, *I will have my car! I will make honor roll this quarter. I will have asked my crush to go to the prom with me by May 1.*

- **Doable goals rely on outcomes that are completely within your control.** If achieving it means others must vote for you, endorse you, hire you, choose you, or say yes to you, rework the goal. *Getting into my dream college* becomes *Meeting the application criteria for my dream college and submitting a strong application.*

- **Visualize and dream about what accomplishing the goal will *feel* like.** By tapping into the emotional connection you have with a goal, you increase your chances of reaching it. Whether you do this by visualizing it while you're lying in bed, by writing in your journal, or by creating a beautiful vision board, explore the outcome you are hoping for.

7
STEP 6: DO THE WORK

When I interviewed screenwriter Susannah Grant of *Erin Brockovich* fame for my book *In Their Shoes*, I asked her what it took to be a successful screenwriter. I'll never forget her answer. She told me, "A lot of people say they're screenwriters, but they don't ever get around to finishing something. Everybody can do it, but the writers are the ones who actually do." The same can be said for doing, well, just about *anything*. No matter how much brainstorming, planning, scheduling, dreaming, and scheming we make time for, without actually taking action and *doing*, To Dos are gonna stay on the To Do list.

It Takes All Kinds

In my life-coaching business, I help people create whatever they want to create in their lives. Consequently, clients ask me all the time to share with them my secrets for sticking to my plan and actually getting things done. And while, sure, I have some techniques that are an essential part of my Doable process, more important than copying someone else's strategies is understanding your *own* personal style for doing and accomplishing things. So really, the key to knowing how you can best get things done is understanding both your strengths and your weaknesses when it comes to taking action.

The reason it's worth knowing this isn't so you can spend time trying to get better at the things you have a hard time with—it's so you can design an approach for getting your stuff done that plays to your strengths. Like we talked about in chapter 4, self-knowledge is the key to it all. There is no right or wrong . . . only *information*. And when we have solid intel about ourselves, we can focus on doing things in alignment with our natural gifts and tendencies. And that, my friends, eliminates frustration, fruitless efforts, and wasted time. The doing part becomes more painless (and even fun).

Sir Ken Robinson knows all about different styles for getting things done. He's a world-famous author who is passionate about education reform. When speaking to large audiences, he often shares the story of Gillian Lynne. As a young girl growing up in the 1930s, Gillian was a problem child at school—so much so that her mother took her to a doctor to be evaluated for a learning disability. The problem? She couldn't sit still in class.

After Gillian's mother told the therapist what was going on at school, the therapist asked to speak with the mother privately, leaving young Gillian alone in a room with music playing in the background. As soon as they left the room, Gillian got up out of her chair and started moving to the music. She just couldn't help herself. As the grown-ups observed this through a crack in the door, the doctor turned to the mother and said something along the lines of, "Your daughter doesn't have a learning disability. Your daughter is a dancer." That doctor couldn't have been more spot on.

Gillian's mother took her to dance lessons, and Gillian was a natural. She eventually went on to become a renowned choreographer, making her mark on Broadway musicals including *Cats* and *The Phantom of the Opera*.

This story is a powerful reminder that sometimes our talents and gifts can be disguised or hidden. Sometimes, like with Gillian, they even look like faults. Instead of tapping into these assets, we focus on all the things we're doing wrong or what we should be doing better. So what does this have to do with making things doable? It relates because the key to fully embracing the action component of your goals is knowing—and accepting—how you work best. It all comes down to Doable styles.

What's Your Doable Style?

There are tons of different ways to learn more about who you are and how you approach tasks. Formal assessments like Myers-Briggs, Kolbe, and StrengthsFinder 2.0 all involve answering a series of questions to categorize you into types as a way to better understand yourself. Gretchen Rubin, *New York Times* bestselling author of *The Happiness Project*, has recently created her own categories—Upholders, Questioners, Rebels, and Obligers—which describe the way people approach things and why.

These are all interesting and insightful ways to explore your own natural tendencies, and if you visit my website you'll find links for learning more about each one. But I've come up with my own types of action styles—fourteen of them to be exact—that define the many different ways people tackle their To Dos. Please note that these are not mutually exclusive—you'll probably see yourself represented in multiple styles.

Read through and carefully consider each one, looking for clues that will help you piece together and identify your own personal action style. Likely, you'll find three to five of these that ring true for you—that's great. Together they'll add up to a clearer picture of your ideal conditions for being your most successful, productive self.

PROFILE YOURSELF

As you go through the list on the following pages, take some notes in your journal or Doable workbook.

1. Which Doable styles do you relate to?
2. What are the associated Doable tips for each one?

When you're done, download your own cheat sheets for every Doable style at www.debbiereber.com. Print out your top tips and keep them handy to apply to all your tasks!

The tips are geared to help you proactively defend against the challenges you may face as a result of your tendencies, and more importantly, they'll help you take advantage of your style's gifts.

SHORT SPURTER

Short spurters work in small, highly productive bursts. For these people, sitting down and toiling away on a project or To Do for long stretches feels tantamount to torture.

Instead, short spurters are able to give a task their complete, undivided attention for little chunks—from five to thirty minutes—before needing to completely switch gears and step away. This may seem like an unconventional approach, but in the end, short spurters are able to chip away at their goals with a cumulative effect of accomplishing whatever they set out to do. Though short spurters can be highly productive, they sometimes struggle when they aren't able to maximize their work periods due to lack of preparation or because they are on such a tight deadline that they must work longer than their ideal in order to get things done.

Doable Tips for Short Spurters

- Plan ahead by gathering and organizing what you need in order to make your short bursts super productive. You don't want to waste time prepping or collecting materials when you might only have a few minutes to do your thing.

- Take advantage of little windows of time that might be great opportunities for your bursts. Things like waiting for the bus, downtime at work, study hall, and sitting in the reception area at the dentist's office are all opportunities for you. Think about times when you might be able to sneak in five or ten minutes of active work toward a goal, and take full advantage!

- Know what your big-picture schedule is, and set concrete and time-sensitive mini-goals to make sure your short bursts will eventually add up to completion.

I defy the stereotype of an author toiling away at the keyboard for hours each day because I myself am a short spurter. My spurts might last fifteen minutes, twenty if I'm lucky. And then I get out of my chair, get a glass of water, fold some laundry, snuggle with my cat . . . basically do anything other than write. And then after some time passes I start the whole cycle all over again. It might not seem like the most efficient way to write, but sixteen-plus books later, I can attest that it works!

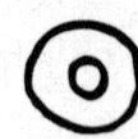

LONG STRETCHER

Long stretchers are the opposite of short spurters in that they thrive when they have big chunks of time set aside to work on goals and To Dos. For these Doers, getting into the mind-set they need to be in to be truly productive takes a while, so the more time they have to focus on a project in one sitting, the more they will accomplish. Long stretchers might get so engrossed in what they're doing that getting them to shift gears or step away from what they're working on takes some persuading. The challenge for long stretchers? Sometimes they won't even get started on a project if they don't feel they have a big enough chunk of time available to them.

Doable Tips for Long Stretchers

- Prioritize your goals or To Dos by clearing space in your schedule for work periods of two to three hours or more.
- Be vigilant about protecting these long stretches of time by eliminating any and all distractions so you can do your thing with ease.
- Don't forget to practice simple self-care while working—bathroom breaks, nutritional snacks, yoga stretches, deep breaths—to best support yourself as you work toward your goal.

DEEP FOCUSER

The close cousin of the long stretcher, deep focusers are people who get completely absorbed in whatever they're doing and are adept at tuning out distractions or outside noises that might disrupt their flow. Similar to long stretchers, it can be hard for deep focusers to notice what's going on around them. They can usually focus on the task at hand in just about any environment, which gives them a lot of flexibility when it comes to pursuing their To Dos. The challenges for deep focusers lie in the reality that their single-minded, focused pursuits sometimes result in their forgetting about other important things, like eating, bathing, going to sleep, and so on.

Doable Tips for Deep Focusers

- Use outside tools or resources for reminders about things going on in the outside world and beyond the scope of your To Do, such as a smartphone alarm to signal that it's time to go to dance rehearsal or your BFF's BBQ.

- Give friends and family a heads up that you're going into focus mode so they don't think you're ignoring them when they call or text you and get no response.

- Think creatively about when and how you can use your ability to tune out the outside world to make true progress on your goals.

Emily-Anne Rigal is a deep focuser when it comes to her passion projects. When she first started We Stop Hate, she says, "I worked on it all the time, and I just squeezed in my schoolwork. We Stop Hate was my whole life, like it was really what I was so passionate about. Building it and creating it was definitely the most fun part about We Stop Hate, having the idea and then seeing it come together. It was amazing. So I would spend hours a day on it, but because I enjoyed it, it didn't really feel like a lot of work."

EASILY DISTRACTED

Easily distracteds are exactly what you think they are—people who can find just about *anything* more interesting than whatever they're supposed to be doing. Easily distracteds might put off setting aside time to focus on their goals or To

Dos, and then once they finally do get down to business, they often struggle to stick with it for more than a few minutes at a time. In this way, they can overlap with short spurters, with the primary difference being that easily distracteds tend to reluctantly show up to their tasks and fight themselves the whole way through the process.

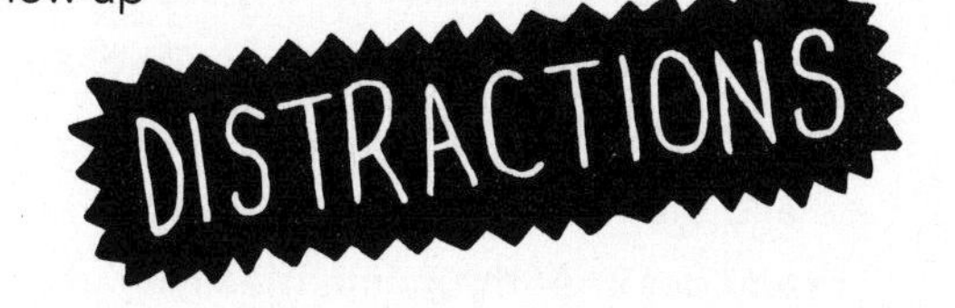

Doable Tips for Easily Distracteds

- Unless your To Do involves your smartphone, put it down . . . in another room . . . with the volume and vibrate off. Same goes for your computer. And your iPad. And any other electronic devices. If you must be on a computer, stay away from social media like it's the plague (unless, of course, your task focuses on social media!). There are a number of online tools you can install or download to help you tune out virtual distraction, including Self-Control, which helps you block out distracting websites for a certain period of time, and Anti-Social, which specifically blacklists your social media time sucks.

- Experiment with different ways to tune out the outside world. For some people, noise-canceling headphones work like a charm; for others, soft classical music might be the ticket. Keep exploring different strategies for eliminating noise distractions until you hit on one that works.

- Be sure you have everything you need with you when you're finally ready to focus. Just like you would before leaving for a road trip, get prepped for your focus time. Go to the bathroom, grab a snack and some water, make sure you're dressed appropriately, and gather whatever you'll need. If after you get started you remember something else you need or want, try writing it down and then working through the urge to stop everything and get it. At this point, it's all about impulse control. And the more you practice it, the easier it will be.

Believe it or not, Google Science Fair winner Naomi Shah classifies herself as an easily distracted, as she feels pulled in so many different directions—school, homework, swimming, research—that it's hard to focus on one task at a time. Her strategy? Compartmentalizing. "In school, I focus on getting the grades. When I'm swimming, I'm not thinking about anything else. I'm only thinking about swimming. In science research, I'm only working on that—I don't have my school email open or my textbook with me."

RAMPER UPPER

Ramper uppers are all about the prep work. Unless they've taken the time to research, prepare, gather, ponder, and get every single duck lined up in a row, they have a hard time getting down to business. Ramper uppers tend to be serious planners, in part because they're trying to eliminate the possibility of doing something wrong that might cause them to fail. Though their prep work helps them feel confident in plunging ahead on any given goal, ramper uppers can sometimes become paralyzed and struggle to take action when circumstances or deadlines make doing extensive prep work an impossibility.

Doable Tips for Ramper Uppers

- Give yourself the time you need to do your prep work, but set limits by picking a target date for eventually taking action. And then stick to it!
- Use your powerful prep skills to your benefit by coming up with a solid and detailed plan for ticking off your tasks as you work toward achieving your To Dos.
- Remember that some things simply can't be planned for, and that's okay. The world won't end if things don't unfold exactly as you'd hoped or if you get thrown off course. Just regroup, think of the detour as helpful information, and get back to work.

CLIFF DIVER

Cliff divers are pretty much the opposite of ramper uppers in that they tend to plunge right in without testing the water temperature, or the depth—or even bothering to look for rocky outcroppings between the cliff top and the clear water below. Unlike ramper uppers, cliff divers don't necessarily see the point in spending valuable time planning—they'd much rather skip the formalities and just get started doing what needs to be done. The challenge for cliff divers is that forging ahead without a clear plan often creates more work and frustration in the long run.

Doable Tips for Cliff Divers

- Embrace the energy behind your action style and find ways to harness it. With focus, your go-get-'em energy can propel you all the way across the finish line.
- When you're getting ready to dive in, consider taking a small amount of time to create a simple plan for pursuing your goal. Even a little bit of prep work added to your enthusiastic process can be a winning combination!
- If setbacks do occur due to lack of planning, take a big step back, regroup, and get set for another plunge. Setbacks can be transformed into lessons learned, so you'll be more likely to succeed next time.

When I interviewed Cammy Nelson of Rep Your School—Build a School, she self-identified as a cliff diver. She explains, "My action style is usually to get really excited really quickly about something and just start immediately and do it as soon as I can. Let's say I find an opportunity on the internet to be some kind of representative for an organization that I'm passionate about and want to work with. So I immediately sign up and register or do what I can." She's had to learn to slow herself down sometimes, though. "One time when I became the president of an organization, I decided to take the position because no one else was volunteering. Other people obviously saw what I wasn't seeing at the time. I took it and then realized the next year that I had bitten off more than I could chew, so I had to renegotiate a few things in this position. That was definitely one time I jumped in before I knew what I was getting into."

SHOOTING STAR

Shooting stars are distant cousins of cliff divers because they too tend to plunge right in with brilliant, exciting energy. But like the meteors they're named after, shooting stars burn out quickly, struggling to maintain momentum and keep moving ahead. As a result, they can be great at getting started with goals and To Dos, but their track records for actually seeing them through can be less than stellar.

Doable Tips for Shooting Stars

- Explore the reasons why you think you burn out and neglect to complete your goals (refer to chapter 4 to help you through this exercise) so you can proactively come up with a plan for getting past the point where you usually bail.

- Look for ways to build accountability—to someone or something outside yourself—into your approach. Outside pressure can be a great way to push through and get to the other side of your fizzling interest.

- Give your momentum a boost by coming up with an enticing reward system or other external motivators. Looking forward to celebrating your accomplishments in a fun and meaningful way can be a helpful carrot to keep you going!

DEADLINE CHASER

Deadline chasers *thrive* on deadlines. Whether because of an innate sense of responsibility or being overly concerned about letting others or themselves down, deadline chasers will stick to a deadline like a fly to tar paper. Most of the time, this is fantastic news—their ability to chase and meet deadlines serves them well. The challenges for deadline chasers are making progress on goals or To Dos where no deadline exists, and making sure self-care isn't neglected in the pursuit of hitting a certain date.

Doable Tips for Deadline Chasers

- Use your deadline responsiveness to your advantage by creating deadlines where there are none. Self-imposed deadlines are often enough to keep you moving ahead. Sarah Cronk of The Sparkle Effect constantly invents deadlines, especially with ambiguous projects—she swears by this method.

- Don't let your dogged ambition to meet your deadlines result in overload and burnout. Practice self-care habits to maintain balance in your life, even when you're up against the wire.

- Be flexible. Target dates are fantastic tools to keep you on track toward your goals, but beware of setting deadlines that are too ambitious or unrealistic. Sometimes deadlines are hard and fast (as in the case of college applications), but sometimes there can—and should—be wiggle room, especially when your well-being and sanity are at stake.

College student Sahar Osmani absolutely considers herself a deadline chaser. As she told me, she's all about calendars and To Do lists. "I have to see it, I have to know that I have to get it done by this time, and then I cross it out when I'm done. It's kind of like that whole quote of: 'To be early is to be on time, to be on time is to be late, to be late is to never show up.' I kind of try and use that with my work, whether it be school, ROTC, or Coaching Corps."

COLLABORATOR

Collaborators are at their best when working with others. They feed off the creative and inspirational energy of those around them, and teaming up with one person, a small group, or a big bunch of people often brings out their best performance, sparks their best ideas, and yields the best possible results. Some goals and To Dos—like climbing Mount Rainier or being part of a winning cheer squad—are literally built for collaboration, which obviously works in these people's favor. But when a task is something that must be done by an individual only, collaborators can feel a bit lost in the process.

Doable Tips for Collaborators

- Choose the people you want to collaborate with wisely to ensure the best possible outcome for your goal. Resist the urge to accept just any help, and focus on identifying key people who can best support you in the way you need.

- Trust in your own ability to get things done even if no ideal collaborators are available. You are creative, resourceful, and whole just as you are. Other people on your team are just icing on the cake!
- When reaching out to others for help or support, be as specific as possible about what exactly you'd like them to do. While many people are eager to help, without a clear road map of what you need from them and why, some might go rogue, do their own things, and end up creating more work for you in the long run.

We Care Act cofounder Grace Li definitely falls in the collaborator camp, considering she founded her nonprofit with her siblings. Grace has this to say about the power of collaboration: "I think individuality is really important. But on the other hand, if you want to accomplish something on a large scale, I think it's really important to have collaboration. Everyone has different connections. Everyone has different ideas. When you have a lot of people working together, you can bounce ideas off each other. You can start with one idea and you can improve. Everyone is constantly improving because everyone has different input."

SOLO WARRIOR

Solo warriors like to go it alone. They plan alone; they work alone; they plug ahead alone. Input from others might make them feel stressed out, judged, or pressured to perform or succeed. They'd much rather have their own space and work at their own pace in their quests to accomplish their goals. Solo warriors tend to be deep focusers and, when given the room they need, can often home in on what has to be done and make great progress with little effort. Their challenge is not knowing when or how to ask for assistance in situations where such help would result in the best possible outcome.

Doable Tips for Solo Warriors

- Find environments that best allow you to do your thing without the possibility of others' energy or input coming into play.

- Be aware of your tendency to take on too much when there are parts of your goal that could be made easier by tapping into friendships and other relationships. Burnout is a real possibility for solo warriors, and asking for help can prevent it. If it feels uncomfortable to collaborate with others, try doing it on something small first to build up your collaboration muscles.

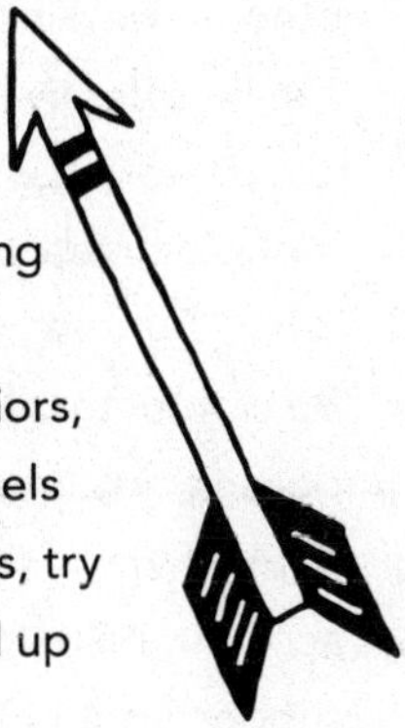

- Know that you're not alone in liking to work alone. In fact, in her book *Quiet: The Power of Introverts*, author Susan Cain writes about how working in solitude often yields tremendous creative results!

ACCOUNTABILITY SEEKER

Accountability seekers like being held accountable to something other than themselves. When they work on a goal, they seek out individuals, groups, organizations, and even formal reporting systems as accountability partners. You might think of accountability seekers as people who are prone to positive peer pressure, in that the expectations of others are enough to spur them on to accomplish their To Dos. This works when a To Do can be easily supported by check-ins, but sometimes accountability seekers struggle to see something through if no one is keeping tabs on their progress.

Doable Tips for Accountability Seekers

- Consider creating a small mastermind group—a group of friends or acquaintances who mutually support each other in working toward goals. Your mastermind group can be effective even with as few as two people as long as you both have a clear understanding of expectations for holding each other accountable.

- Be careful that your desire to meet others' expectations doesn't result in being overly focused on what others think of you, as this is a slippery slope. Positive accountability from others comes from a place of honest support, not judgment. Ultimately, only you get to decide what completing or not completing your task means.

- Connect with automated or virtual accountability systems that allow you to mark your progress without relying on another person. For example, use an online To Do list system or make your own star chart (remember those from preschool?) so you can see your progress. You can also create a success wall in your bedroom

where you post sticky notes that highlight targets and deadlines that you met.

SCHEDULER

Schedulers love order, plans, and timelines . . . a lot. For schedulers, knowing exactly how and when something is going to be executed takes the stress out of the equation (or at least lowers it significantly). Schedules also give them a clear path that increases the likelihood of reaching their goals, provided of course that the schedules they created in the first place were realistic. Schedulers are superb at organizing, which will take them far. However, when outside forces throw a wrench in their finely laid plans, it can be difficult for schedulers to regroup.

Doable Tips for Schedulers

- Set mini-deadlines for each small step that leads to reaching your big goal. This will keep you on track so you can move ahead smoothly.

- Create realistic timelines for everything on your To Do list. If you think you've budgeted enough time for a particular step, consider doubling it, and then do that for each additional step along the way. Falling behind schedule can be tricky for you, but being ahead of schedule is no problem whatsoever. So build in wiggle room and you'll be more apt to enjoy the feeling of a job well done . . . even early!

- Get creative when it comes to scheduling your tasks. Use smartphone alerts and reminders, online calendars, whiteboards, or even virtual To Do lists on your computer, tablet, or phone. There are many resources designed to help people meet deadlines, and guess what—you're the ideal user for them!

REWARD JUNKIE

Reward junkies are highly externally motivated. Dangle a carrot in front of them—a bigger allowance, extra privileges, an award at school—and they'll put their Doable efforts into full throttle. Reward junkies like to receive praise and to feel acknowledged for what they've accomplished, not to mention to reap the fruits of their labor. But reward junkies don't have to always be focused on something they can get from the outside world. Oftentimes, creating a personal reward system works just as well. The important thing is noticing and celebrating when a task or goal has been achieved, even if that acknowledgment occurs in a very simple way. Things get tricky for reward junkies when their desire to receive an outside reward outweighs their personal desire to achieve the stated goal.

Doable Tips for Reward Junkies

- Watch out for situations where an outside reward becomes intertwined with your stated outcome for a goal. Goals with results that are dependent on anything outside yourself are out of your control and inherently less than ideal. Make sure your hoped-for outcome is fully within your control, and consider the reward, if you receive it, to be an added bonus.

- While you're enjoying your reward after a job well done, take time to acknowledge to yourself what you've accomplished. Notice how good it feels to follow through on something, how proud you are of your accomplishment, and the steps you took to reach your goal.

- For tasks that don't have overt reward systems built in, find ways to create little personal rewards for yourself to fulfill that need for external motivation.

INTRINSICALLY MOTIVATED

Intrinsically motivateds are polar opposites of reward junkies in that the majority of their motivation and inspiration comes from within. Intrinsically motivateds value personal responsibility and have an innate sense of follow-through. They do things in large part because they like the way it feels to do them and to get them done. They sometimes challenge themselves to take on bigger and bigger tasks because the thrill of pursuing a goal and the joy of reaching it are all the motivation they need. While there are no big challenges for intrinsically motivateds, they may be overachievers, and therefore can be tough on themselves when they don't accomplish their goals as quickly or as perfectly as they'd hoped.

Doable Tips for Intrinsically Motivateds

- Slow down and enjoy the *process* and not just the achievement—you learn and grow a lot during the journey!

- Allow yourself to enjoy rewards when they do come your way. Rewards don't take away from your accomplishment or make your pursuit of it less meaningful—they're just an added bonus!

- Celebrate your innate sense of intrinsic motivation—it's considered a trait of highly successful people!

So, where did you see yourself? Remember—there is *plenty* of overlap here. Chances are you're a blend of multiple styles. You might be a cliff diver + accountability seeker + reward junkie, or a ramper upper + solo warrior + scheduler. Me? I'm a short spurter + ramper upper + accountability seeker + scheduler + reward junkie. The bottom line: No matter what you are, *it's absolutely perfect*. There's no right or wrong, no good or bad, no judgment. It's really all about self-knowledge. It's about understanding how you best do things so you can get out of your own way, set yourself up for success, and start kicking some serious booty!

Do the Work

So now you have a handle on your own Doable style as well as tips for capitalizing on your strengths. You can set yourself up with the best possible circumstances so you can thrive in your quest to pursue your goals and To Dos. But there's one more thing you need to do in order to cross that finish line and get to the other side of your goals. It's quite simple really . . . just three little words: *Do. The. Work.*

There's no way around it. Just like screenwriter Susannah Grant said, "Everyone can write, but writers are the ones who actually do." Writers write. Runners run. Entrepreneurs create. Unless we chip away at our goals and To Dos by actually *doing*, we'll never finish what we started. So make your goals and To Dos a priority. Create a mind-set around action and push to reach your accomplishment.

You've got this. I just know it.

STEP 6 SUMMARY

Every single person is capable of getting stuff done. I don't care if you have trouble finishing things, or you flit about from one idea to another, or you're about as organized as a typical toddler—you have it within you to commit to something, plan how to do it, and then actually do it. When you understand your own personal Doable styles, you will be able to confidently claim (or reclaim) your identity as someone who *does* things, and you will set yourself up for success.

Step 1: Define Your To Do 

Step 2: Detail the Little Tasks 

Step 3: Defend against Obstacles ☑

Step 4: Develop Support Systems 

Step 5: Determine What Success Looks Like 

Step 6: Do the Work

Goal setting, planning, dreaming, and scheming are all well and good, but unless you actually get down to the business of *doing*, you'll never actually accomplish anything. Doing is all about taking action—getting started, taking those first steps, and finding a way to keep the momentum up through the finish line. To be your best action-oriented self, remember to:

- **Take time to consider your own strengths and weaknesses when it comes to getting things done.** Choose strategies for taking action that play to your strengths (of which you have many), and eliminate strategies that don't come as naturally to you.

- **Get familiar with your own Doable style.** With this knowledge, you can understand your ideal conditions and circumstances for being your most successful, productive self, and find ways to take advantage of the great parts about how you work. If you're a short spurter, steal moments to make progress when you're waiting for the bus or sitting in the reception area at the dentist. If you're a deadline chaser, set personal deadlines even where there are none, and so on.

- **Three words: Do the work.**

8
STEP 7: DEAL WITH SETBACKS

You might be wondering why, since the previous chapter was all about finally buckling down and getting work done, I'm now throwing in a chapter about *setbacks*. And I get it. I mean, here you've got all this great momentum going and I come along and remind you of the possibility that things may not go as planned.

Well, I've got good reason to do so, and this is it: in every hero's journey, there are challenges and setbacks (and yes, *you* are the hero of your story). There just are. No matter how finely planned a pursuit, *something* is bound to go wrong along the way . . . it's just part of the deal. Ask Michael Jordan, who got bumped from his high school varsity basketball team, or Oprah Winfrey, who lost a hosting gig early in her career because someone thought she wasn't "fit for television," or Bill Gates, who dropped out of college, or John Grisham, whose first novel was rejected by sixteen agents and twelve publishing companies. The list of famous failures goes on and on, but you get the point: everyone struggles; everyone fails sometimes.

Cammy Nelson noticed that setbacks were a regular part of trying to get her nonprofit, Rep Your School—Build a School, off the ground. *No* was apparently the word of choice as Cammy worked her way up the university hierarchy of administrators trying to get the green light so she could turn her idea into reality.

"I don't usually burst out in emotion, but when I get really frustrated or upset, I handle it by having a minor breakdown and crying a lot. That's just how I've always been whenever I get really frustrated. So there were a lot of tears shed—I was just so frustrated with people not seeing the same potential of the program that I did. And so I remember one night sitting on my campus calling my parents because I was like, 'I don't know what to do anymore.' I just wanted it to happen because I believed it would be good." But Cammy didn't let that stop her. "I handled it by setting up another meeting. I just thought, *This isn't going to stop here.* So I sent another email and set up a meeting with the people who eventually said yes. I guess I handled those setbacks by getting overwhelmed and then letting it go and then taking the next step. But there were lots of tears shed," she says.

So, failures and setbacks? The reality is, there's a very good chance they will happen to you. Maybe not today, maybe not during the particular goal you're chasing right now, but at some point, it's gonna happen. And when it does, your default reaction may be feeling uncomfortable, scared, disheartened, frustrated, or simply like a big old failure. But here's the thing about setbacks: if we can persevere and remind ourselves of our intentions, those setbacks may not only get us where we want to be but also make the whole journey more meaningful and rewarding when we're on the other side.

What's So Bad about Failure?

So, what exactly is it about failure that strikes fear into the hearts of so many people? And since when did failing become something so terrible that people try to avoid it at all costs, even if that means never trying to do anything worthwhile in the first place?

Like everything else in life, it's our thoughts and beliefs about failure that form the basis of our relationship with it. The reality is, without our assigning some sort of meaning to our failures, they would just be circumstances. You know, instead of making our failures mean something about who we are—*I'm not good enough, I'm not smart enough, I'm not talented enough, I just don't have what it takes*—when something goes wrong, we'd simply shrug our shoulders and say, "Oh, bummer . . . that happened." And we'd move on.

Here's the thing about failure: the very act of putting ourselves out there and taking risks that might involve failure is a *positive* thing. As author and researcher Brené Brown says, "When failure is not an option we can forget about learning, creativity, and innovation." Plenty of highly successful people, from entrepreneurs and engineers to businesses executives and athletes, credit their failures for their ultimate successes. Business tycoon Richard Branson—who has experienced many high-profile failures in the midst of his successes—says, "If you're going to fail, fail hard, fail well. It simply means success is just around the corner." He knows that refusing to risk failure means refusing to tap into your true power and genius. And how unfulfilling would that be?

Still, failing can be tough. And learning how to handle setbacks, disappointments, and failures takes practice. But just like anything that involves moving outside your comfort zone, it gets easier with practice. And ultimately, you'll get to a place where you can see a setback as an acceptable outcome, just part of the process, *no big deal*.

The Art of Failing

So how exactly does one deal with unexpected setbacks when working toward a goal? How can you get from the *ugh* of disappointment to the other side, where you can reengage with the goal from a more empowered place? Let's walk through an example to take a closer look at the process.

Say Kaitlyn is trying to memorize one of Muzio Clementi's sonatinas to play in the school talent show in May. She's never entered the talent show before, but this year she decided to take a risk and share a part of her that her friends don't usually see. And hey, if she happens to impress a few folks along the way, in particular a senior named Sebastian, all the better.

Kaitlyn has used all the Doable steps so far to help her pursue her goal. She has:

1. **Defined the To Do:** Play Sonatina in C Major, op. 36, no.1 by Clementi by memory at the talent show on May 7.

2. **Detailed the little steps:** Get the sheet music, sign up for the talent show, come up with a realistic practice schedule, practice each movement separately *with* the music every day, start trying to do parts of it by memory, build the amount played by memory versus looking at the music over time, have three practice performances for friends and family in the week prior to the show, get

a good night's sleep the night before the show, kick butt at the performance!

3. **Defended against obstacles:** Kaitlyn recognizes her tendency to get distracted with other things when she's feeling pressure mixed with a lack of confidence, and she proactively came up with a defense strategy to combat her usual distraction tendencies.

4. **Developed a support system:** Kaitlyn told her big sister what she was trying to do and asked her to watch TV downstairs instead of in the living room so she could practice without interruption. She also recorded herself playing so she could listen to the music while playing it as a way to nail the notes, and she scheduled extra sessions with her piano teacher to get tips for memorizing music.

5. **Determined what success looks like:** Kaitlyn is super clear on how she'll know when she has achieved her goal—performing the piece at the talent show without any major screwups. She's even been visualizing herself successfully playing the piece, calmly and confidently.

6. **Done the work:** Kaitlyn has been sticking to her schedule and has figured out that she's a short spurter + easily distracted + scheduler + reward junkie. She has set herself up for success by making the appropriate tweaks to her plan to capitalize on her strengths.

But . . . then something happened.

Kaitlyn held one of her practice recitals. Two days before the show. For an audience of three (Mom, Dad, and Sis). Four if you count the dog.

And . . . she *totally choked.*

Halfway through the second movement, fingers flying staccato across the keys, her mind suddenly went blank. And then she panicked. And then she just stopped playing, a deep grumbling weight filling the pit of her stomach. She tried to pick up where she left off, but she just couldn't get her rhythm going again. Face red and feeling defeated, she pushed herself away from the piano and slunk up to her room.

That might not seem like such a big deal to you, but for Kaitlyn, her faux-recital failure ended up being a *major* setback. As she lay in bed that night, she found herself unable to visualize the happy, confident image she'd been focusing on in the previous weeks, and instead, she started to imagine the absolute worst. The thoughts running through her head sounded something like this:

- *I'm going to completely humiliate myself.*
- *Everyone will think I'm a total loser.*
- *I never should have signed up for the talent show in the first place.*
- *My reputation will be ruined if I screw up, and I'll never recover.*

As you can imagine, thinking these thoughts isn't really fodder for confidence, and focusing on them will likely cause Kaitlyn to either pull out of the talent show altogether or show up to the event a bundle of nerves, play her song with shaky hands, and possibly do the exact same thing during the performance that she did during the practice run.

So what's the alternative? To reframe the situation and consciously change the chatter in her head about what went wrong and what that means. It's easier than it sounds . . . trust me.

Shift Those Thoughts!

For Kaitlyn to get back on track for accomplishing her To Do, she needs to shift her thoughts to generate a positive, supportive new reality. The same is true for all of us, and it only takes three steps:

1. **Accept that setbacks are part of the deal.** If we believe that a setback is *terrible* or *awful* or *unacceptable*, then setbacks and failures become something we fear and avoid at all costs. And then when things do go wrong, we give those setbacks so much weight that they throw us into a tailspin . . . one that just might be unrecoverable. But if we accept the fact that setbacks are part of trying to do *anything*, they become just another part of the process. Even better, they can become an important factor in bringing us closer to our ultimate goals.

2. **Experience the emotions tied to setbacks and failure in a healthy way.** Disappointment, frustration, and sadness are all completely appropriate and normal emotions when something doesn't go our way. But some people let those emotions take over; they awfulize the situation by dwelling on the negatives. They slip into a dark place

of shame and despair. On the flip side, there are people who don't want to deal with any of the uncomfortable emotions at all, and they shove the feelings deep down and suppress them. That isn't a healthy option either, as it can lead to chronic health problems, unhappiness, and in some cases, depression. The secret is letting the emotions wash through us—notice them, acknowledge them, feel them, and then let them go.

3. **Ask questions to explore and discover the reality of what's going on.** Try starting with these: *What can I learn from this situation? What is the worst thing that could happen, and can I survive it? What changes can I make to my plan based on this new information that will better enable me to reach my goal?* Inventor Thomas Edison supposedly said, "I have not failed. I've just found ten thousand ways that won't work." So, what didn't work that you could tweak or shift to see if you'll get a better result? How can you modify your goal to incorporate your new reality?

Kaitlyn could do a little DIY Coaching here by first reminding herself, *Hey, mistakes happen. Even great pianists have screwed up in the middle of big, live performances.* (It's true.) Putting yourself out there and taking big risks, like playing piano in the school talent show, isn't easy and may feel seriously uncomfortable, but when Kaitlyn accepts that mistakes may happen and realizes that's totally okay, it doesn't feel like as big a deal.

Next, Kaitlyn could have a little freak-out. She could allow herself to feel and process all those emotions: embarrassment, dread, and the fear that she'll make a fool of herself at the show. She could notice if she's emotionally spiraling out of control and fixating on super big and extreme thoughts along the lines of *I'm setting myself up for the biggest catastrophe of my life!* and remind herself of what she already knows: in reality she will survive whatever happens, and she can get through anything.

Lastly, Kaitlyn could take a step back and ask herself some questions about what happened to discover what really went wrong so she can learn from the setback and move forward armed with new insight and confidence. Here's what that process might look like for Kaitlyn:

- **What went wrong?** *I completely blanked in the middle of my song, froze, and couldn't get back on track again to finish.*

- **What is my biggest concern?** *I'm worried I'm going to make a complete fool of myself at the talent show if the same thing happens there.*

- **What can I learn from it?** *When I'm feeling nervous, there's a good chance I'll lose my focus, and if I lose my place in the song, I might not be able to pick back up where I left off and complete the piece. Although professional pianists perform with no sheet music, maybe I'm not at that stage yet. Maybe I'm being too hard on myself by thinking I have to hold myself to a standard of perfection.*

- **What changes can I make to enhance my chances of success?** *I can ditch the idea of playing the piece by memory and have my Clementi book with me. I'll ask Maisie to sit on the piano bench next to me and turn pages.*

Now Kaitlyn has a new plan for pushing ahead and performing in the talent show—one that feels more achievable and less stressful, thank you very much. Sure, she still might flub some measures in the piece, but she'll be able to get back on track easily as long as she has the music with her. And had she not had that setback in the practice recital, she might not have made the adjustments to her plan that, in the long run, made achieving her goal that much more doable.

DIY COACHING: SHIFT THOSE THOUGHTS AND EMBRACE FAILURE

When was the last time you experienced a setback or a failure while working toward a goal? Turn that failure into self-knowledge and an opportunity to be more successful next time by doing a little DIY Coaching:

1. Accept that the setback was simply a part of your goal-getting journey. It is what it is—nothing more, nothing less.

2. Allow yourself to experience the emotions tied to the setback or failure in a healthy way. Don't ignore them, and don't fixate on them—just notice, acknowledge, feel, and release.

3. In your journal or Doable workbook, honestly explore thoughtful questions about what happened. Questions to explore include:

   - What went wrong?
   - What is my biggest concern?
   - What can I learn from it?
   - What changes can I make to enhance my chances of success?

The Mid-Goal Blues

Losing momentum and feeling insecure or unmotivated about a pursuit doesn't only result from a big failure or setback. Sometimes, midway to a goal, you lose steam for other reasons. You might start to doubt your ability to complete what you're working on, or you might start to feel disconnected from your Why for doing it in the first place. You might just get tired—physically, mentally, emotionally, or all of the above—and start to question your intentions. Or things may not be unfolding exactly as you'd hoped, and you may feel like throwing in the towel.

If this has happened to you, please pay particular attention to this next sentence. *This is normal.* That's right. Everything I've just described is completely normal. It doesn't mean you can't finish anything. It doesn't mean you aren't committed anymore. And it doesn't mean that you should give up.

More than likely, it means you're stressed, you're overtired, or your life is out of balance, whether as a result of goal pursuing or not. Our bodies let us know that something is off by feeling tired, disconnected, insecure, or unmotivated. We're supposed to take notice of those signals and do what it takes to address whatever is going on. If the signal tells us we're running on fumes, then we need to notice that and think about ways to get more rest. If the signal tells us we're out of touch with why we're working so hard, then we need to reset our intentions and take steps to remember what we hope being successful will look and feel like.

This is something Sarah Cronk of The Sparkle Effect has faced a lot over the past several years. As I mentioned earlier, Sarah cofounded The Sparkle Effect because she felt passionate about including special needs students at her school. As a member of the cheering squad at Pleasant Valley High School, she was able to reap all the benefits of what she was creating. She was personally touched by the experience she was helping bring to students with disabilities. It was profound and impactful.

But now Sarah is in college, and though she still runs The Sparkle Effect, she's no longer regularly hanging out with the students who benefit from the organization. She's no longer getting to experience those feel-good vibes on a regular basis.

"One of the hardest things for me was transitioning from running my own Sparkles team at my high school to doing all the work without experiencing all the rewards—you know, the internal rewards. That was tough at first." But Sarah got through the mid-goal blues. "I had to push through it and understand that what I am working toward is bigger than the day-to-day. So now it makes me just as happy to see that another team has started and that they're experiencing what I used to experience in my high school. Even though I don't get to be there for the start of that team [and] I don't often get to be at that first practice, I get to imagine the smiles on their faces and how excited and happy they are."

When I asked Sarah how she boosts her spirits when she is feeling disconnected or down, she told me her secret. "Sometimes for me it means pulling up a video of me with my team when I was in high school, flipping through a Facebook album of when we were all together, or going back and watching old videos of teams. When I just really don't want to fill out that grant application or something like that, I take a break for like ten, twenty minutes, go down memory lane, look at that old stuff, and just let myself feel refreshed and reenergized," Sarah explains.

The Benefits of Failures and Setbacks

As you can see, changing the way we think about the setbacks we encounter makes all the difference when it comes to whether or not those setbacks will be positive or negative experiences for us. Remember, *you* get to decide how you feel about your setbacks. So why not choose to view them in a positive light? Here are some more helpful ways to consider failure in case you're not quite convinced:

Failure is feedback. Nothing more, nothing less. Failure is *information* that tells us something isn't working or there's a better way. And when you think about it, isn't this information exactly what we need to get us closer to reaching our goals?

Failures and setbacks build ***grit,*** which is defined in the *Oxford Pocket Dictionary* as "courage and resolve; strength of character." The more setbacks we face, the more grit we build. The good news here? According to Paul Tough, author of the *New York Times* bestseller *How Children Succeed,* having the qualities of grit and perseverance are much more important in determining future success than things like good grades or compliant behavior. In fact, research shows that people who *didn't* have to overcome obstacles as kids are actually less happy as adults. (Hmmm . . . makes you think about failure in a whole new light, doesn't it?)

At this point, I think it's fair to say that teen researcher Naomi Shah has built up enough grit to get her through a lifetime. She has logbooks highlighting all the things that went wrong in her experiments so she can work through the problems. So what does she do when setbacks occur? She dives in. "I am totally fine with cold-calling professors or professionals in the industry and asking questions. Just sending out ten or eleven emails that night and saying, 'I'm a high school researcher. You don't know who I am, but this is what I'm working on and here's a problem I ran into. Could you help me work through it, and could you help me figure out a reason why this is happening?' I've learned that it's okay to look stupid or not as smart, because at the end of the day, it's progressing your research and getting to your goal that matters. Usually people don't think you're stupid for asking a question. They think that you're bold or you're taking action to get to your goal."

And that, my friends, is what grit looks like.

Failure results in creativity. True innovation—the kind that can literally change the world and the way we live in a positive way—is often the result of failure. When something doesn't work out as planned, it challenges people to push themselves to come up with creative solutions. You can bet your bottom dollar that any society-changing invention or technological advancement throughout history came about after, or possibly because of, multiple setbacks and failures.

Failure begets self-knowledge. When things go wrong, you have the opportunity to examine your response to the setback and explore your own ideas and thoughts about failure. Why does this matter? Because how we experience adversity tells us a lot about who we are, how we see the world, and how we see ourselves fitting into it. And that kind of self-knowledge will help us get through everything in life. In her 2008 commencement address at Harvard, author J. K. Rowling talked about her own failures in this regard: "Failure taught me things about myself that I could have learned no other way. I discovered that I had a strong will, and more discipline than I had suspected; I also found out that I had friends whose value was truly above the price of rubies."

As in the example with Kaitlyn's performance in the talent show, failure often happens while you work toward a goal. Since so many of our To Dos involve multiple steps, there are obviously multiple opportunities for things to go wrong at any point along the path. When they do, dive into DIY Coaching to shift those thoughts and embrace the failure so you can deal with the associated feelings, course correct, and move on. To be a Doable goal-getter, you have to know that you won't make it every time, and that's okay. Life is about trying things. It's about going for it. It's about the journey.

STEP 7 SUMMARY

I hope that by now you're convinced that failing is not only part of the deal but also most likely a positive thing. Anytime I start to question this notion, I think of my favorite office supply, the beloved Post-it. It never would have been brought into existence had its creator, 3M, not failed epically by developing a glue that didn't stick very well. While that glue may not have created an unbreakable bond, it was the perfect thing for the back of a note you want to stick somewhere but still be able to move from place to place. Yes . . . failure can totally suck, but if you can see it as just another (necessary) step toward your goal, you can deal.

Step 1: Define Your To Do 

Step 2: Detail the Little Tasks 

Step 3: Defend against Obstacles 

Step 4: Develop Support Systems

Step 5: Determine What Success Looks Like  

Step 6: Do the Work 

Step 7: Deal with Setbacks
Expecting, embracing, and learning from the failures and setbacks you face along the way is one of the most powerful steps in the Doable process. Mastering this step will serve you well

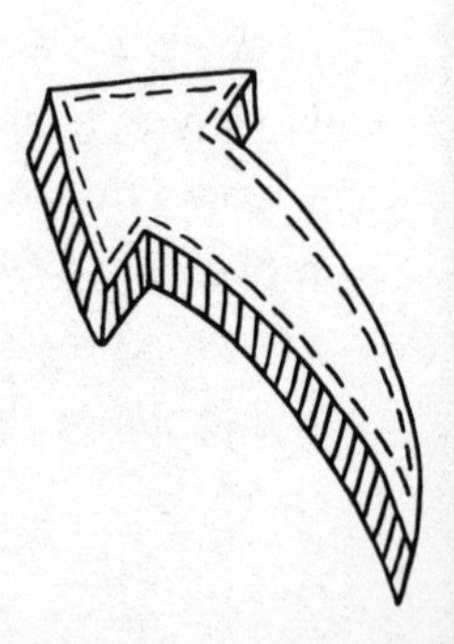

throughout your entire life and will allow you to experience your Doable journey in a more meaningful and rewarding way. Here are some things to keep in mind when you're facing setbacks and failures:

- **How you feel about your setbacks and failures is solely determined by what you think about them.** You get to *choose* what your failures mean. Keep it realistic! *I'm not good enough* or *I just don't have what it takes* become *Oh, bummer . . . that happened.*

- **Shift those thoughts and embrace failure rather than struggle against the undertow:** 1) Accept that setbacks are part of the deal (Kaitlyn reminded herself that mistakes happen); 2) Experience the emotions tied to setbacks and failure in a healthy way (Kaitlyn allowed herself a small freak-out while not going over the edge); 3) Ask yourself questions to explore and discover the reality of what's going on (Kaitlyn asked questions that led her to the realization that memorizing the piece was too much pressure, and she changed her plan, making it more doable).

- **Understand the many, and very real, benefits of failures and setbacks.** Failure is feedback—it builds grit, it results in creativity, and it begets self-knowledge. All of these are good. *Really* good.

9

STEP 8: DELIVER THE GOODS

In the past seven chapters, we've worked our way through the Doable process and explored how to apply each step to your goal. By now, hopefully you've gotten clear on what you want to achieve, made a plan for doing it, proactively set yourself up for success, lined up external support, figured out how you'll know when you've accomplished your goal, buckled down to the serious business of *doing*, and likely faced (and hopefully overcome) a few challenges along the way. But for everything we want to do, there comes a point when we've reached the end of the journey. That's what the last Doable step, Deliver the Goods, is all about.

Each time you commit to a task or a goal, there are several possible outcomes. You can:

- **Achieve it:** This is the golden ticket—it means you've accomplished your goal as you stated it. Boom.

- **Change course:** Sometimes you decide, in the middle of the whole process, that you don't want to accomplish the goal after all or that your purpose has changed or evolved. So the original goal isn't relevant any longer.

- **Fail to achieve it:** Sometimes you just aren't successful in reaching your goals or achieving your To Dos. It happens. You survive and go on.

All three of these options are outcomes you'll likely experience in some way, shape, or form many times throughout your life. The reasons why could depend on the goal, what's happening in your world at the time, and many other factors. So let's take a closer look at what each one looks like and how you can best experience it. Because no matter the outcome, there is something to be gained from the experience when you take the time to reflect.

Achieving the Goal

Well, this is really what we're all going for, right? To identify something we want in our lives (whether it's a change, an opportunity, a tangible object, or a big result), come up with a plan for making it happen, and at the end of the process, succeed in doing exactly what we set out to do.

Achieving your goal, no matter how big or small, mundane or earth shattering, is a *big deal*. That's right. You made a decision to do something and then *you did it*. And that's all on you. Sure, you may have had help along the way, but at the end of the day, you are the one who stated your goal and then had the wherewithal to see it through to completion. And that, my friend, is something to celebrate, whether that looks like dancing around in your underwear to Katy Perry, having a girls' night out with your friends, or simply enjoying a toast from your family at dinner. Plainly put, celebrating feels good and is a wonderful way to bring a Doable journey to a close.

But there's a deeper reason you shouldn't skip your celebration. By truly acknowledging your accomplishment, you can max out on all the positive energy your achievement has created. Because when you accomplish a goal, you get so much more than just the tangible benefits of the accomplishment. You also get momentum, confidence, and the creation of new neural pathways—meaning your brain works better and success will be even easier next time.

YOUR BRAIN ON ACCOMPLISHMENT

In his *New York Times* bestselling book *The Power of Habit: Why We Do What We Do in Life and Business*, author Charles Duhigg talks about how reaching goals, even small ones, can propel us toward bigger, more significant accomplishments: "A huge body of research has shown that small wins have enormous power, an influence disproportionate to the accomplishments of the victories themselves." This means that each time we achieve something, no matter the size or importance, we gain motivation and inspiration that will help us pursue future goals with even more confidence. So it only makes sense that we'll be even more likely to reach those future goals as a result.

If you look up the most successful entrepreneurs of our time, you'll see that they didn't just come out with one big idea and strike gold. Jeff Bezos of Amazon and Richard Branson of Virgin, arguably two of the world's wealthiest entrepreneurs, both started out small and built their businesses over time through a series of small successes. Even Mark Zuckerberg, who appeared to come out of nowhere when he created Facebook, had a long history of pursuing and accomplishing many goals, including developing computer games and taking graduate courses while still in middle school, being the captain of his high school's fencing team, and being courted by AOL and Microsoft before he even graduated from high school, not to mention the fact that he was accepted to Harvard (no small feat). With every little thing Zuckerberg worked toward and accomplished, he gained *momentum* to keep him moving forward and taking risks. He was having experiences that led to new experiences. Zuckerberg, like Branson and Bezos, was on his own personal cycle of Doability.

A positive side effect of all this momentum building is *confidence*, which can be defined as a feeling of certainty or truth about something. When we feel confident in our abilities to do something . . . *anything* . . . we embrace our certainty about what the outcome will be from the get-go. In other words, confidence enables us to work toward goals with the assumption that we will ultimately achieve them. Confidence locks in a positive mind-set, which shapes what our goal pursuit will look like, making it much more likely that we'll reach our goals.

I like to think of confidence as a muscle. For example, imagine your triceps muscles. You don't pay much attention to them until you try to do a push-up and realize your arm strength is pretty much nonexistent. But then you struggle through a few knee push-ups one day and a few more the next, and as the days go by, you gradually add more muscle. Before you know it, you can drop and do twenty at a moment's notice. Once you start flexing and building your confidence muscle, this can-do attitude will soon become part of how you show up, both to tasks and to the world.

Because of her successes in creating and building her blog, Ella Viscardi feels über-confident about the future. "Now I have this background that really can show other people who I am and where I'm coming from, like my specific voice. I definitely am really interested in working in the fashion industry when I'm older, and I know it's not an easy realm to get into, but just the fact that I've been having this blog and it's made me learn so much about fashion already, I do feel like I have some knowledge about technology and writing and just the world of fashion to bring with me into whatever I do next. It definitely makes me feel confident," she explains.

For Tammy Tibbetts of She's the First, sometimes the smaller tasks and To Dos play as big a role in building her confidence as accomplishing the big goals. A self-described former perfectionist, Tammy often reflects on something her first boss once told her: "Don't let perfection get in the way of better." In her quest to let go of perfection and build her own confidence muscles, Tammy puts a priority on exercise.

"I sometimes feel incompetent with tasks I have to do for She's the First because I haven't mastered the new skills, but then I think, *Well, you felt that way about yoga four months ago and look at you now. You're not too bad.* So I think it's important to give yourself other outlets for other goals. Maybe it's not a fitness goal, maybe it's a goal for how to play an instrument or something. But it's important to work on things outside the realm of whatever the main project is because, even if you don't realize it, you're going to be making [neural] connections that will reinforce you."

Brain science gives us clues as to how acknowledging our achievements might help cement our success-oriented outlook and increase the likelihood of positive outcomes for future tasks. We all have neural pathways in our brains, which are essentially little nerves that information travels along. Our neural pathways determine how we experience everything, and like deep ruts in a road, these pathways can become firmly etched in our brains. *Unless* we consciously etch new ones.

Say you are someone who hasn't always seen things through to completion. Maybe you've crashed and burned a few times and you are convinced you're the queen of self-sabotage. You likely have some deep ruts in your neural pathways that support this mind-set and negatively influence your likelihood of success. But what if you challenged some of those beliefs about your self-sabotage and decided to pursue your goal in a new way—a way that yielded some awesome results? Choosing to think differently and to try a new approach forms new neural pathways. Do it again, and again, and you'll eventually find you've created new ruts in the road—you'll have shifted your mind-set to one of success and optimism. And which mind-set do you think is going to result in a more positive outcome for future tasks and To Dos?

ACHIEVING THE GOAL . . . ALMOST

One more thing I think is important to consider before we move on: achieving your goal doesn't have to look perfect. Sometimes you reach the conclusion of your quest with slightly different results than you'd hoped for or predicted.

Say it's your senior year and you're bound and determined to get your best time ever swimming the 200-meter freestyle.

All season long, you stuck diligently to the training schedule your coach devised to make sure you peaked during the state championships. When the time comes for the big race, you're well-rested, your body is perfectly fueled by ideal foods, and your lane assignment is number five, which just happens to be your lucky number. Yet, despite swimming your heart out in optimal conditions, you fall short of beating your best time of 2:07.99 and instead finish in 2:10.74. You still place in the top ten—better than you've ever placed before—but if you'd actually beaten your best time, you could have been on the medal stand for the first time in your high school career. And all because of three lousy seconds.

So, what to do? Technically, you didn't meet your goal of setting a personal record, but for all intents and purposes, you were successful in your pursuit and execution of it. You did everything you could do to make it happen, but it just wasn't in the cards for you that day.

So what does that mean? Should you retire your Speedo, hang your head in shame, and mope around like a big failure? Are you any less just because you failed to blow past your old record? Methinks not.

This circumstance I just described, the one where you get super close to a much sought-after end result but don't quite reach it? Yeah. This happens. *A lot*. And the worst thing you could do is believe that since you didn't meet your goal exactly as you'd hoped, then it doesn't count at all. Well, that just isn't true. This outcome does not mean you failed. When near misses like this happen, I suggest treating them like a *win*. That's right. Pat yourself on the back. Celebrate your tush off. And acknowledge the fantastic efforts you undertook as you worked toward your goal.

REFLECTION

Whether you achieved your goal or you had a near-miss conclusion, take some time to debrief about your Doable style.

DEBRIEF

Grab a pen and your journal or your Doable workbook and ask yourself the following questions to see what kinds of insights you can put in your toolbox for the *next* time you chase a goal or dream:

- What am I most proud of about the way I pursued my goal?
- If I could start over and try again, what would I do differently?
- Is there any way I could have made my goal more doable?
- What have I learned about my Doable style that I can use in the future?

For We Stop Hate's Emily-Anne Rigal, reflection means noticing and appreciating not only her own role in an accomplishment but also the role of others in her success. "Along the way, when you're trying to accomplish something, you're not ever doing anything alone. So I think it's so important to recognize that and show people that you're thankful for all they're doing because it's your goal. If you don't appreciate, you can't be happy. The whole point of being successful and accomplishing goals is so that you can feel good about yourself and feel happy." Don't forget to thank yourself, though. "I think it's essential that we all take credit for what we've done," Emily-Anne says. "It's not that I think this all happened because other people did it for me. I think I had a lot to do with it, so being proud of myself and acknowledging what I've done is important too."

Changing Course

While this book is about making anything doable, there will be times in your life when you're plugging ahead on something and then you realize, *Hey, this isn't really something I want to do anymore.* You might consciously choose to change course and take your To Do off the table before you've completed it. This is different from not perfectly meeting the criteria for your goal or not achieving your hoped-for result. No, this is when, for whatever reason, you simply decide you're just not that into the goal anymore.

For example, maybe your goal was to land a job at the movie theater to make extra cash on the weekends, but after you nailed your interview, you realized you'd much rather work a job that will give you your weekend nights free, so you withdraw from the application process. Or maybe you've been preparing for an audition for an exclusive summer theater program, but before the big day comes, you have an aha moment and realize your *real* dream is to take summer classes at the Art Institute.

This is all perfectly good and fine because the reality is, *we are always changing*. It's part of what makes us dynamic, interesting, creative beings. We are constantly absorbing new information, insights, and perspectives and incorporating them into our own opinions and experiences. That information, along with all the other influences in our lives—our friends, families, and the media, to name a few—shapes who we are and how we think about our lives and choices. We are constantly evolving.

Some of us worry about what others will think if we change our minds about a goal. Will they assume we failed? Will they think we couldn't hack it? Will they think we are flaky and can't stick to anything? Maybe. But frankly, who cares? And no, I'm not being cheeky. I mean it. Who cares? It's time to let go of what other people think because, at the end of the day, it doesn't really matter. It doesn't change who we are. Their perceptions of us are not necessarily true. And besides, we can't control their opinions about us anyway. In fact, you could keep pushing ahead and achieve a goal you've completely lost interest in, and other people *still* might think you're flaky. So what's the point of even giving others' perceptions a second thought?

On the other hand, maybe the person whose opinion you're most worried about is *you*. After all, no one is more critical of ourselves that we are. And if you have it in your head that you are someone who struggles to follow through or that you are a classic self-sabotager, you might decide that shifting a goal proves just how bad you are at actually finishing anything. If I just described you, remember that *you* get to decide who you are and how you think about yourself. And therefore, you can choose to not believe that version and come up with your *own* version of the truth. Something along the lines of: *I'm glad I felt confident enough to step away from a goal I wasn't passionate about anymore. I look forward to putting my energy behind something I'm truly excited about and making it happen!*

For author Marni Bates, changing courses means being okay with the fact that the first novel she ever wrote is still sitting under her bed. "It's a great manuscript," she says. "I loved it at the time. But it needs a whole lot of work to ever be published. I see that now. I needed time and I needed distance from that manuscript. And I still look at it with deep, deep affection and love, but if I hadn't set it aside, I wouldn't be where I am. That book was a great launching point for me, but it was my next book that actually moved my career forward. There's no shame in a non-completed manuscript. There's no shame in a half-finished project. It's all about finding that project that really does fit."

Remember this: Changing course isn't failing or bailing. It's evolving and growing. It's all good.

DEBRIEF

Because a change of course often stems from a change in us or our circumstances (or both), it's worth it to take a few minutes to explore the situation by answering the following questions:

- Why did I decide to change course before completing my goal?
- How have I evolved since I first began pursuing this goal?
- What did I discover about myself in the process?
- How can I take what I've learned about myself and factor it in the next time I pursue a goal?
- If I pursue this goal again in the future, what will I do differently?

Failing to Achieve the Goal

The third potential outcome when we're working toward a goal is the one we'd probably rather not even mention lest it come true: flat out not achieving the goal at all. Going back to our examples from previous chapters, this might look like not earning enough money to buy that used car after all, or chickening out about asking the hot crush to prom, or not getting the grades to qualify for honor roll.

When we don't reach a goal, we have a choice. We can look at that failure as evidence that we're somehow *lacking* (not the option I'm advocating!), or we can take a step back, assess what went wrong, and make a conscious decision about how we want to move forward, whether it's starting from square one and giving it another go or deciding it is what it is and moving on. The most important thing to remember is this: There is no shame in not succeeding. None. Zilch. Nada. Because what we do or don't do has no bearing on who we are or how much value we have. What matters is how we show up—how we deal with the failure—and where we go from there. Goal pursuing isn't a zero sum game. *Every single part of going after To Dos and goals has value.* We just have to soak in that value.

So what *does* it mean if you don't reach your goal? Well, it simply means you didn't do it this time. That's it. It means there's an opportunity for you to learn more about who you are by reflecting on your whole journey.

DEBRIEF

Once you've had a chance to recover from the disappointment (this may be a short or a long period of time, depending on the importance of the goal), take a half hour or so to journal your answers to the following questions:

- Despite the fact that I didn't achieve my goal, what part of my Doable process worked well for me?
- If I could start over and try again, what would I do differently?

- Is there anything I could have done differently that would have made me more likely to achieve my goal?

- What did I learn about myself through this process?

- What is perfect about the way this situation worked out? (This might feel like a stretch to answer, but go ahead—stretch and give it a try. If you can't think of anything, email me the situation at debbie@debbiereber.com and I'll help you come up with something. Promise!)

- Do I want to pursue this goal again?

Just taking the time to reflect on these questions will help you shift your perspective and leave you feeling more positive about the outcome, even if it doesn't look like what you were hoping for.

It might not happen right away, but trust and believe in yourself—you will be able to move on from a stronger, more inspired place.

Celebrate You

But enough about what to do when you don't end up where you'd hoped you would. Let's move on to talking about the good stuff, like you making it happen and reaching your goals, because I have a hunch that's going to be your story more often than not.

I first heard the term *shipping*—used to describe delivering the goods or completing a goal and moving on—from author, entrepreneur, speaker, and marketing guru Seth Godin. He writes extensively about this concept, and how all our talk and work and planning isn't worth anything if we're not willing to see something through to the finish line. He describes this on his blog: "In a long distance race, everyone gets tired. The winner is the runner who figures out *where to put the tired*, figures out how to store it away until after the race is over. Sure, he's tired. Everyone is. That's not the point. The point is to run. Same thing is true for shipping, I think."

So, now that you've shipped, *yay, you!* It's time to acknowledge and celebrate your achievement!

Now, you may not think that following through on what you set out to do warrants putting on your party pants, but I'm here to tell you, *you're wrong* (and I say that with the most possible respect). Recognizing your accomplishment is a positive, empowering, joyous thing to do—and it's the final step in the Doable process. Not taking the time to celebrate is kind of like getting a chocolate fudge sundae and asking the server to hold the fudge. Celebrating seals the deal and gives you the opportunity to pat yourself on the back, marinate in your victory, and maybe even receive congratulations from the people around you who are proud of your success.

There are many different ways to acknowledge and celebrate your accomplishments, whether you managed to finally put together the Ikea bookshelf you've had in a box for the past three months or you reached your goal on Kickstarter to launch your nonprofit. Here are just a few suggestions to get you started, but ultimately, how you mark your achievement is totally up to you!

REWARDS

As I wrote in chapter 7, some people are super motivated by the prospect of receiving a reward after reaching a goal. Even if the promise of a reward isn't a driving force while you're actually pursuing a goal, there's no reason why you can't reward yourself after the fact. I mean, who doesn't love a little reward every now and then?

Of course, sometimes the reward is the result of the achievement itself. Take, for example, the teen who was saving money to buy a used car. Her reward after reaching her goal is the car. And that's a pretty great reward. But in cases where the achievement doesn't necessarily equal fun or awesomeness—finishing a research paper or getting all your recommendations in for your college applications, for example—celebrating with a super indulgent reward at the end makes your accomplishment all the better, especially when achieving it was a slog fest and involved a ton of work, energy, and perseverance.

YA author Marni Bates buys herself a commemorative piece of jewelry for each book she finishes. For example, in her novel *Decked with Holly*, her main character gets a pearl necklace, so Marni bought one for herself as a memento of the whole journey. She also bought a bracelet to mark the publication of her book *Awkward*. "It's been really great for me to have something that I can wear and that makes me feel proud of myself when I wear it," she says.

I'm intrinsically motivated, yet I always celebrate my big achievements with rewards, anything from a dinner out with my girlfriends to a massage to an afternoon shopping spree. I enjoy these rewards completely guilt-free because I know I worked my bum off to earn them. They're well deserved, and like the L'Oreal tagline says, I'm worth it.

ACCOMPLISHMENT BOARD

Posting completed To Dos on an accomplishment board is one of my favorite ways to recognize the successful completion of things on my list. What this looks like is up to you, but the gist is this: an accomplishment board is a physical place—a wall, the back of your bedroom door, a bulletin board, a whiteboard, the side of your dresser—where you tack up your accomplishments.

Every time you cross another goal off your list, scribble it onto a sticky note and slap it onto your accomplishments board. Voilà—you have a visual reminder of just how much you've actually done. And each one of those sticky notes represents not only a successful outcome for yourself but also your future potential to tackle anything you dream of. Maintain your accomplishments board and I have no doubt that you'll eventually run out of space. Soon, you'll have to resort to posting new accomplishments over old ones. Don't believe me? Try it.

ACCOMPLISHMENT JOURNAL

Similar to the accomplishment board, keeping an accomplishment journal is another way to document your successes while also giving you the room to capture your reflections and thoughts about the whole process. Choose a journal with a design you love, find the perfect pen, and go to town writing about your successful pursuits of To Dos. At the end, you'll have a valuable documentation of your best practices and insight into your ideal Doable style, not to mention an inspirational and motivational book you can refer to the next time you're feeling less than confident about the goal you're chasing.

For college student Anna Gallagher, writing out her accomplishments is all about coming full circle with her goals. When she's first thinking about goals (step 1), she writes about who she is, who she wants to be, and what makes her happy, and then she only pursues goals that are in alignment with what she just wrote down. So at the conclusion of a project or when she has completed a To Do, she goes back to that list and checks in.

"I like to see if I've done something that's made me happy, that has enhanced who I am, and that has progressed my life in some way. And then I always like to set new goals and have something new I'm working toward. So as soon as I finish one goal, I try to come up with what my next project is, and once again think about how I want to change in the future," she explains.

PHOTO BOOK

Depending on what it is you accomplished, you might choose to create a photo book to fully memorialize your achievement. I know how fabulous these can be because my friend Alice makes them for me every few years—awesome picture books highlighting my successes and achievements. Talk about a confidence boost! If your To Do involves the completion of a

journey or challenge, having images of you along the way and successfully doing your thing will be something you can refer back to for years to come! Even better, simply looking at those images of you—crossing the finish line, paragliding, surfing, doing a ropes course—can instantly create the same feelings in your body that you experienced when you were doing it the first time around. And those feelings, when harnessed in a positive way, are tantamount to your own personal superpower.

SOCIAL MEDIA BLITZ

Part of celebrating and acknowledging your accomplishment might mean telling the world about it and graciously accepting their congratulations. FYI—this isn't being braggy (unless of course your intention is to be braggy . . . then it is). Rather, it's a powerful way to publicly acknowledge what you've done while simultaneously making yourself vulnerable and open to receiving goodness and praise. (Remember what Brené Brown said about vulnerability? Yeah, it's a good thing).

Take it from me—as soon as I wrap up this chapter, I'll be posting on Facebook that I finished writing my book! For me, part of the reward and recognition comes from having my friends cheer me on and give me virtual hugs for reaching my goal. It kind of seals the deal and adds to my feel-good completion vibe. At the same time, it lets the people who care about me know what important things are happening in my world, which makes *them* feel good. Again, win-win. So, if it's your thing, tweet out your good news or update your Facebook status so the world can celebrate your accomplishment. And then you can just sit back and soak up all that good energy.

What You Do Matters

We Care Act cofounder Grace Li knows a thing or two about reflection and good energy. But I'll let her tell you all about it: "Ever since I was a little girl, I always wanted to do something grand, extraordinary. It was only through We Care Act that I realized to do so, you can't just do it by yourself. You have to start a chain reaction. I really love the idea of a chain reaction, now even more so because of what happened when I went to China a couple of years ago with my siblings.

"When we were China, I taught an English workshop there to the Sichuan earthquake victims. At the end of the workshop, the English teacher was standing on the steps of the school when she asked all the students, 'How many of you would like to join We Care Act as a team leader and pay it forward?' Every single student raised their hand. Now they're all active team leaders. They contribute to every project that we do.

"That's really made me realize that so many people out there want to make a difference. For me, I realized that the way to do something extraordinary isn't just by getting into it by myself, but by creating a network chain reaction of people who all want to do the same thing."

What I love about this story? It is a beautiful reminder that what we do matters, whether we're changing the lives of children halfway around the world like Grace does or creating something meaningful, positive, happy, or important in our own lives.

Whatever you're up to, I know you have big things to do in the world. I hope this book has given you some strategies to make every one of them happen. So, I'd better say goodbye and let you get started. Good luck, and keep me posted on your progress. I'm rooting for you!

STEP 8 SUMMARY

Would you ever devour an awesome novel only to toss it aside as soon as you read the climax? Probably not. If you're like me, you'd want to read all the way to the end so you could find out how the characters fared, see all the pieces of the story neatly wrap up, and experience the satisfaction of turning that very last page. This is what the last step on your Doable journey is all about: closing the chapter on your goal so you can make room for a different dream, or perhaps the same dream reworked if you weren't successful the first time around. It's about experiencing a sense of completion and reaping all the benefits of the extraordinary process you've just been through.

Step 1: Define Your To Do ☑

Step 2: Detail the Little Tasks ☑

Step 3: Defend against Obstacles ☑

Step 4: Develop Support Systems ☑

Step 5: Determine What Success Looks Like ☑

Step 6: Do the Work ☑

Step 7: Deal with Setbacks 

Step 8: Deliver the Goods

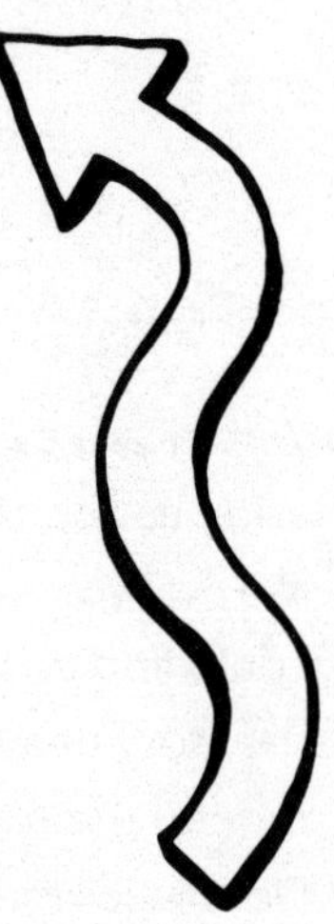

Delivering the goods means seeing a goal—or the pursuit of a goal—through to the end, no matter the outcome. You might not have realized that reflecting on the end of a Doable journey is part of the process itself, but the acts of acknowledgement, celebration, and reflection can offer you beaucoup benefits. Here are some highlights to help you experience your own goal conclusions:

- **Formally acknowledge the achievement of your goal.** This way, you maximize the positivity your accomplishment has put into motion, including momentum, confidence, and the creation of new neural pathways.

- **Treat near misses—goals you pursued beautifully but missed achieving your hoped-for outcome—as wins.** Celebrate your hard work, and then reflect on lessons learned by asking yourself questions like: *What am I most proud of about the way I pursued my goal? If I could start over and try again, what would I do differently? Is there any way I could have made my goal more doable? What have I learned about my own Doable style that I can use in the future?*

- **Give yourself permission to change your mind about a goal.** We are always evolving and changing, and sometimes that means our goals change before we reach them. And that's okay.

- **If you fail to reach your goal, take a step back, assess what went wrong, and decide how to move forward.** You can choose how you think and feel about not reaching your goal. Don't make it mean something negative about you—focus on what you can learn about yourself and your Doable process so you can shift perspective and pursue future goals from a more empowered place.

- **Celebrate you.** No matter how big or small your accomplishment, find some way to formally acknowledge and celebrate with tangible or intangible rewards—an accomplishment board or journal, a photo book, a social media blitz, or whatever ideas you can come up with!

10
HOW *DOABLE* BECAME DOABLE

Each time I write a book, the process looks different. I wrote my novel, *Language of Love*, sunken in my comfy chair in the corner of my Seattle home, feet propped up on the ottoman, notes shoved in the space between the cushion and the chair, and thighs burning up from the heat radiating from my laptop. I had a rhythm, a routine, a goal, and a deadline. I had the tools I needed, a muse (my late dog, Baxter), a support system in place, and a customer card for my favorite frozen yogurt place, which I frequented after hitting target word counts.

I had my process, and it worked.

But writing *Doable* looked very different. For starters, I didn't even own the same big comfy chair, and even if I had, writing in my living room had lost its magic for me. Instead, I was a coffee shop nomad, in search of the perfect spot with the perfect energy and the perfect sugary treats. My schedule was wonky, I had an energetic nine-year-old to take care of, and because of my move to Amsterdam, which happened midway through the first draft, my support system was no longer in my neighborhood, but rather a nine-hour-time-zone-difference Skype call away. Frozen yogurt? It was nowhere to be found.

In order to get this book completed in time, I was forced to adapt to my environment and my situation and discover new ways of working that could keep me on track and moving forward. I had to apply each and every Doable step to my goal of turning in this book on time, which frankly, seemed like an impossible feat *many* times along the way. To show you what it looked like for me, here is how *Doable* became doable:

Step 1: Define Your To Do

My goal at the onset was pretty straightforward: to write my book and complete it by my deadline. And my goal was concrete by design—I knew exactly what I had to do (write the book) and what completing it would look like (emailing a finished manuscript to my editor on time). And despite the fact that there were extenuating circumstances happening in my life that made hitting my deadline challenging, writing and completing the book was 100 percent within my control. Lastly, I was already super clear on my personal Why for writing the book—I wanted to share my passion for dream pursuing and empower young women to achieve their goals. (Woot!)

Step 2: Detail the Little Tasks

I am forever making To Do lists of my mini-tasks, so I'd begun doing this as soon as I knew I was writing this book. My tasks involved things like interviewing girls (which involved tons of smaller tasks like finding said girls, arranging phone interviews, conducting the interviews, transcribing the interviews, and so on), researching, and writing and editing multiple drafts. Because I'd been through this process before, I knew what writing a book entailed, so this made detailing the tasks a pretty straightforward process for me. I was working on a tight deadline, so I set target dates for a number of my mini-tasks, including when I wanted to have all my interviews completed and when I planned to finish both my first and my final drafts. I'm a scheduler, so I stuck to these targets and stayed on track.

Step 3: Defend against Obstacles

At this point in my life, I am pretty chummy with my obstacles, which for me tend to involve both being distracted and feeling like I don't have enough time to get it all done. With *Doable*, both of these obstacles were related to and magnified by the reality that I was coordinating an international move, which left me dealing with real estate closings, yard sales, packing, dealing with shipping companies, and adjusting to a new life in a strange land right in the midst of my writing process. I proactively defended against both of these obstacles by trying to get ahead of schedule in anticipation of the craziness to ensue, and cutting back on as many commitments as I could so I could focus on the one big goal I was working toward. Lastly, I used DIY Coaching to come up with my new truth, which was this: I always hit my book deadlines. My new truth was true, and every time I started to freak out (yes . . . it happened more than once), I repeated that truth. *I always hit my book deadlines.* Then I took a deep breath and got back to work.

Step 4: Develop Support Systems

Boy, did I ever embrace this step! I needed help, big time, and I asked for it. First I asked my parents if they would help me pack up my house during my last weeks in Seattle, while I was conducting phone interviews with the most impressive young women I've ever met. My parents happily flew out from the East Coast to help me out. (Have I mentioned that my parents totally rock?) Then, once I got to Amsterdam, I immediately signed up with a babysitting service so I could have some coffee shop writing time to wrap up my draft. Boy, was that a relief. And when I needed accountability, I asked three fabulous friends—Gia, Jen, and Elise—to check in on me and make sure I hit my target dates. Plus, like I wrote earlier in the book, I'm a fan of using Facebook pressure to spur me on. For me, it works. Lastly, after transcribing one and a half of the ten interviews I conducted and realizing it would take me hours and hours to get through them all, I put out a call for transcription help and within twenty-four hours had emailed the rest of my interviews off to a service, enabling me to focus on writing.

Collaboration

Step 5: Determine What Success Looks Like

This one was easy for me. I knew exactly what success looked like: sending an email to my editor by my deadline with my completed manuscript attached. As far as what it would feel like? One word: *relief.*

Step 6: Do the Work

Like I wrote earlier in the book, getting stuff done is one of my gifts. I am very aware of my Doable style—short spurter + ramper upper + accountability seeker + scheduler + reward junkie—and I used this self-knowledge to ensure I would reach my goal. I took advantage of every possible short window of opportunity to get work done (short spurter), I did all the prep work and research before I started to write (ramper upper), I built in systems of accountability through friends and Facebook (accountability seeker), I set clear target dates for the tasks associated with my goal (scheduler), and I frequently rewarded myself with frozen yogurt, long walks, and naps (reward junkie).

Step 7: Deal with Setbacks

I've had many failures and setbacks over the years, and I can honestly say that when they do happen, they don't negatively impact me much anymore. Through much coaching, I've come to accept that setbacks are always going to be part of my journey and therefore they don't take me long to recover from. In the course of writing *Doable*, I didn't have any major writing setbacks—no hard drive crashes or deleted chapters. Rather, my biggest setback stemmed from losing my dog Baxter while writing this book. I couldn't eat, or write, for about two weeks during that time, so I got a little off schedule. But instead of judging myself and getting upset, I reminded myself of my new truth again—*I always hit my book deadlines*—and let it go.

Step 8: Deliver the Goods

Well, I guess because you're holding this book in your hands, it's no surprise that I delivered the goods. I turned in my manuscript on time (twelve hours early, even!) and lived to tell about it. To formally acknowledge my goal, I called my friends and family to share the good news and give them the chance to congratulate me (that felt good for all of us), and I posted a note on Facebook. A few nights later, I went out on a date with my husband to celebrate, which felt well deserved and all-around awesome. I reflected on my journey by making some blog posts and writing in my journal. And I suppose even writing this chapter (I added this section after the rest of the book had already been written!) is a form of reflection as well. Oh, and one more thing . . . I caught up on sleep. Lots of it.

From To Do to Done

As you can see, it wasn't necessarily easy, but having been through the process of creating and doing and delivering many times before, I trusted in my ability to capitalize on all my strengths to *get it done*.

I invite you to trust in yourself the same way. No matter what your track record is for reaching goals and checking off To Dos, you are someone who can *get things done*. I swear, it's true. Just like me, you have to adapt as you and your life circumstances change, and you have to figure out new ways to thrive when old ways don't work anymore.

Trust me when I say that's perfect . . . that's the way life is. It's only when we remain rigid about the way things supposedly should be that we lose out on how awesome they *could* be—how awesome *we* could be—if we just got comfortable pushing ourselves outside our comfort zones, taking a few risks here and there, and figuring out who we are. You have it within you to do anything you want to do. So play around with the Doable steps, dig in to self-discovery work, experiment with different strategies, and *be curious* about yourself and your process. Do, notice, learn, adapt, move forward, and do again.

In the beginning of *Doable*, I told you I wrote this book to help you be as productive as you want to be . . . to turn any goal or pursuit into a doable venture. There's more to that, though. The truth is, I wrote it because I believe you are remarkable, self-aware, and generally kickass. I believe in you and what you are going to create with your life and for the world.

But no one knows you better than you. My hope is that this book has given you even more insight into the ways you can use all your brilliant talents, skills, and strengths so you can get stuff done on an epic level.

So, are you ready to start *doing*?

ACKNOWLEDGMENTS

Anyone working toward a big goal benefits from having an awesome community of people in her corner, and that was definitely the case for me as I wrote this book.

To my wonderful agent, Susan Schulman, who believes in what I do and my passion for young women. I am so grateful to have you in my life!

To the fantastic team at Beyond Words Publishing, including acquiring editor Nicole Geiger who first championed my book, developmental and production editors Ali McCart and Emmalisa Sparrow, managing editor Lindsay Brown who took this book up a notch in every way; interior designer Sara Blum who brought the content to life so beautifully; and Jackie Hooper, Whitney Quote, and Leah Brown, for their passion for marketing and promoting *Doable*.

Thanks to my fabulous Simon Pulse family, including Bethany Buck, Mara Anastas, and Patrick Price, as well as designer Karina Granda for her cover design.

I loved getting to know the kick-ass young women I featured in *Doable* and am thankful they took time out from changing the world to share their stories with me: Marni Bates, Sarah Cronk, Anna Gallagher, Grace Li, Camryn Nelson, Sahar Osmani, Emily-Anne Rigal, Tammy Tibbets, Naomi Shah, and Ella Viscardi.

I have some of the most incredible people on my virtual "support team," including AnneMarie Kane, Alice Wilder, Ed Adams, Renée Adams, Alison Bower, Mardi Douglass, Sara Gersten-Rothenberg, Gia Duke, Mia Michaux, Kayce Hughlett, Elise Touchette, Jen Trulson, Marci Davis, and David and Barbara Basden. You all are a part of this book being birthed.

I couldn't have written this book without my (late) beloved dog Baxter, who served as my muse, my companion, and my office mate, and will always hold a piece of my heart.

I'm beyond grateful for Dale and MaryLou Reber, aka pops and mom, who are there for me anytime, anyplace. (Little known fact: these fabulous people flew across country to help me pack up my Seattle house pre-move and watch my son so I was free to interview the girls featured in this book.)

Oodles of thanks to my sis and BFF, Shelly, my go-to gal for the great stuff and the hard stuff and everything in between. I couldn't ask for a better sister and friend.

And most of all, thanks to my main squeeze Derin, who, let's face it, makes what I do possible, and my mini-main squeeze Asher, who keeps me grounded and living in the moment. There's no one I'd rather be with on this journey.

ALSO BY
DEBORAH REBER

So how is this goin 2 work?